The Abstracted Vine A Guide to Grapes, Regions & Real-Life Pairings for Those with a Wandering Mind

This book is dedicated to my loving and encouraging family and friends who helped me along this winding vineyard and brought my love of wine to life! And to Charlotte Brown for the most beautiful cover art.

Diana xo
Thank you for
everything
Audrey

First Printing, 2025

The Abstracted Vine A Guide to Grapes, Regions & Real-Life Pairings for Those with a Wandering Mind

Aubrey Graf-Daniels

CONTENTS

1

Introduction

Wine is ancient.

It's libation and sacrifice, celebration and sorrow, pleasure and prayer. It's liquid history—a living, breathing alchemy of culture, nature, and time.

We've been making wine for roughly 6,000 years, give or take a few centuries. Why? Because, once upon a time, wine was safer to drink than water. From the slopes of Georgia to the temples of Egypt, through the Levant, India, and China, wine traveled along the spice routes and seafaring empires—Phoenicia, Greece, and Rome—before becoming a core part of the Western winemaking tradition.
France, Italy, Spain, and later, the so-called "New World": The Americas, Australia, New Zealand, and South Africa. Every bottle today carries echoes of that journey.

So... What Is Wine, really?

Technically, wine is fermented grape juice. But not just any juice. If you crush grapes and leave them alone, something magical happens. The natural yeast clinging to their skins wakes up, feeds on the sugar in the juice, and transforms it into alcohol and carbon dioxide. That's fermentation. That's wine.

Grapes + yeast + time = wine. Simple. And yet, infinite.

The sweeter the grapes (think sun-soaked vineyards or late harvest fruit), the more sugar there is to ferment—meaning more alcohol and often a fuller body. Grapes from cooler climates, or picked early, bring less sugar but more acidity, usually leading to wines that feel crisp, zippy, and refreshing. This delicate balance—between sugar, yeast, and time—shapes the wine's aroma, flavor, body, and soul.

And here's where it gets fun for the wandering mind: This is just the beginning.
The chemistry of fermentation is a doorway.

Step through, and suddenly you're exploring why Pinot Noir thrives in Burgundy but struggles elsewhere, or how volcanic soils in Sicily change the flavor of Nerello Mascalese.
You start to see that wine isn't just what happens in the glass— it's a conversation between climate, grape, place, and time.

Wine is history you can taste, science you can sip, and culture you can share. It's proof that something as ordinary as a grape can, with patience and a little fermentation, become extraordinary.

A Note from the Author

Look, I have ADHD. If a subject doesn't captivate me, I drift off like the bubbles in Champagne. My mind zips to a dozen other things—half-finished projects, new ideas, or that random lyric stuck in my head. But wine? Wine keeps me grounded. Wine keeps me engaged. It's not just memorization—
It's sensory, experiential, alive. It gives me something to hold, smell, taste, and question. It's learning with all five senses, and for me, that makes all the difference.

I'm not here to lecture or to drown you in flashcards.

I'm here to offer a reference, a map, a path—one you can return to, flip through, and sip alongside. Something that welcomes tangents, because wine is full of them. Every glass is a branching trail: history, science, culture, memory.
You get to decide which path to follow.

Why Learn About Wine?

Why not?

Wine brings people together. It starts conversations, sparks debates, enhances dinners, and binds us to land, story, and memory. It's a bridge—between you and your senses, between you and the people you share it with, between you and centuries of tradition.

And it invites you to ask questions—the kind of questions curious, wandering minds thrive on:

What grape is this?
Where did it grow?
Who made it—and why?
What's hiding beneath that aroma of cherry or spice?

Each bottle is a curiosity loop, a puzzle box, an invitation to explore.

For those of us with ADHD (or just an unquenchable thirst for discovery), wine is the perfect subject: limitless, sensory, and ever-changing. It rewards short bursts of attention as much as deep dives. You can learn a little—or fall headlong into an entire rabbit hole of grape varieties, volcanic soils, or medieval trade routes. Both are valid. Both are fun.

How to Learn About Wine (Without Losing Interest)

Start small. Start sensory. Pour a glass and taste it slowly. Take notes (or don't). Draw doodles. Jot down colors, moods, or even song lyrics that the wine reminds you of. Create your own system using color-coded journals, voice memos, or sticky notes on the fridge. Use an app if that works for you. Or don't and just let the memory of the moment stick in your mind like a snapshot.

Pair wines with music, with weather, with a meal, with the people around you. See how it changes when you're outside vs. inside, with friends vs. alone. Wine is not a subject you conquer. It's one you live alongside. You don't have to "study wine" to love it. You just have to show up, sip, and let it speak. Because for a wandering mind, the beauty of wine is that it never runs out of things to say.

The 5×5 Starter (ADHD-Friendly)

Wine can feel overwhelming—too many grapes, regions, rules. The 5×5 is your

shortcut: five simple anchors to keep you curious, engaged, and in the moment.
No memorization required. Just pause, sip, and play.

5 seconds: Pause, look, swirl.

Take a moment before diving in. Hold the glass. Notice the color. Watch how it clings to the side. Give it a swirl and let oxygen unlock the aromas. Those five seconds create space for your senses to catch up with your attention.

5 senses: Sight, smell, taste, touch, sound.

Sight: Notice color—pale straw vs. deep ruby can hint at grape, age, or style.
Smell: Stick your nose in. Aromas are memories in disguise.
Taste: Sweet, sour, salty, bitter, umami—your palate is a compass.
Touch: Is it silky, gritty, or fizzy? Texture tells a story.
Sound: Don't underestimate the pop of the cork, the fizz of bubbles, the gentle pour—it all sets the stage.

5 words: Rapid descriptors.

No pressure, just gut reaction. "Citrus, saline, peach pit, fresh, light."

Or "jammy, bold, oaky, cozy, autumn."

Five words anchor your experience without overthinking.

5 sips: Layers of discovery

1. The first sip calibrates your palate.
2. The second show's structure—acid, tannin, balance.
3. The third reveals the finish—how long the flavors last.
4. The fourth is with food—does the wine click or clash?
5. The fifth is just for fun—because pleasure is part of learning.

5 comparisons: Build a frame of reference.

Compare across bottles, vintages, and winemaking styles.

Ask: How does this wine differ from the last? Does a cooler site make it sharper, more electric? Does oak soften or sweeten? Every comparison sharpens your palate and adds context without cramming facts.

Over time, you may find that wine isn't just something to drink— It's something to follow

like a thread running through culture, language, memory, and identity.
Wine is social glue and a sensory playground—perfect for curious, wandering minds. It's hands-on, ever-changing, and forgiving: You don't have to "get it right." You just have to show up.

So, grab a glass, try the 5×5, and let's explore the world of wine— one sip, one question, one delightful tangent at a time.

2

Italy

Regions of Italy
Trentino-Alto Adige
Lombardy
Valle d'Aosta
Friuli-Venezia Giulia
Trento
Milan
Vicenza
Venice
Veneto
Piedmont
Turin
Adriatic Sea
Bologna
Emilia-Romagna
Liguria
Florence
Marche
Tuscany
Umbria
Abruzzo
Corsica (France)
Molise
Rome
Lazio
Puglia
Naples
Sardinia
Tyrrhenian Sea
Campania
Basilicata
Ionian Sea
Calabria
Sicily
Palermo
Mediterranean Sea
Copyright: The Society of Wine Educators 2019

3

Northern Italy

Piedmont

Famous For: Barolo, Barbaresco (Nebbiolo). Think dark cherries, truffles, and royal-level tannins.

Barolo was once referred to as "the wine of kings, the king of wines." It was so highly prized that it became the currency of the royal court.

Nebbiolo means "little fog," and the region's famous wines (Barolo, Barbaresco) get their name from the mists that roll in each autumn.

Notable wine producers in Piedmont:

Gaja: A world-renowned producer with a significant annual output, known for its Barbaresco.

Bruno Giacosa: Another iconic producer with a large annual production.

Giacomo Conterno: A historic, traditionalist winery with a highly sought-after Barolo.

Massolino: A prominent producer located in Serralunga d'Alba, known for its high-quality wines.

Vietti: A historic winery whose Barolo wines are highly respected.

Mascarello: A legendary figure in Nebbiolo, whose legacy continues to be celebrated.

Pio Cesare: A long-standing and well-known winery in the Barolo region.

Produttori del Barbaresco: A cooperative known for high-quality Barbaresco.

Fratelli Revello: A winery recommended for its quality.

Azelia: A fifth-generation winery known for producing precise and highly sought-after wines.

Lombardy

Famous For: Franciacorta (Italy's Champagne rival), Bubbles, lakeside lunches, and alpine elegance.

Franciacorta is made exactly like Champagne, but Italians aren't allowed to call it that. It's Italy's most elegant sparkling secret. **Franciacorta spends more time aging on its lees than Champagne**—some producers let it rest for 60 months!

Top wine producers in Lombardy include Guido Berlucchi, Ca' del Bosco, and Bellavista for Franciacorta sparkling wines, along with Ca' dei Frati for Lugana and white wines. Other notable producers mentioned are Ar.Pe.Pe, Casa Vinicola Aldo Rainoldi, and Conti Sertoli Salis in the Valtellina region, and several others in the Oltrepò Pavese area, such as Azienda Agricola Barbacarlo di Lino Maga.

Trentino-Alto Adige

Famous For: Pinot Grigio, Lagrein, Gewürztraminer, white wines with zip! Reds with altitude attitude.

German-Italian fusion — in grapes and culture.

With over **100 grape varieties**, this "dual-language" region has more grape diversity per square mile than almost anywhere else in Italy.

Top Producers in Trentino-Alto Adige:

Cantina Tramin: A leading cooperative known for high-quality white wines, especially Gewürztraminer and Chardonnay.
Foradori: A renowned producer, particularly praised for its Teroldego reds and the Manzoni Bianco white wine.
Tiefenbrunner: Frequently cited as a top producer in the region.
Cantina Terlano: A highly-regarded winery with a reputation for quality.
Franz Haas: Recognized for high-quality wines, including a Pinot Noir that has been considered one of the best in Italy.
Alois Lageder: Another producer frequently mentioned among the region's best.
Elena Walch: A prominent producer in the Alto Adige.
Weingut Loacker: A respected organic producer. Cantina di La Vis e Valle di Cembra: An important cooperative in the region.

Veneto

Famous For: Prosecco, Amarone, Soave. Whether you prefer fizz or bold, it's wine for every mood.
Prosecco is the most exported Italian wine in the world. More than **600 million bottles** are exported globally every year.

Renowned Producers in Veneto:

Quintarelli Giuseppe: A historic and highly regarded producer, particularly famous for its Recioto della Valpolicella Classico and Amarone della Valpolicella.
Allegrini: Another leading name in the Valpolicella region, celebrated for its high-quality Amarone.
Bertani: Known for producing excellent wines from various appellations, including Soave and Amarone della Valpolicella.
Tommasi: A well-known producer of Amarone della Valpolicella.
Sartori di Verona: A prominent producer with a long history in the region.

Friuli-Venezia Giulia

Famous For: Orange wines, Friulano, Sauvignon Blanc. Natural wine lovers, start here. Orange wine central! This region helped revive skin-contact white wines before they became trendy. **Friuli was the first Italian region to adopt grape varietal labeling in the 1970s.**

Pioneering and Renowned Producers in Friuli- Venezia Giulia:

Josko Gravner and Radikon: These two producers are icons of the region's modern winemaking movement, pioneering extended skin contact for white wines and aging in amphorae.
Jermann: A legendary producer, famous for wines like the "Vintage Tunina," known for their quality and longevity.
Mario Schioppetto: A visionary figure in Italian enology, his namesake winery continues to produce high-quality, structured, and long-lived wines, particularly from Sauvignon Blanc.
Livio Felluga: A historic and respected name in the region, known for producing a wide range of high-quality wines.

Liguria

Famous For: Vermentino, Pigato Cliffs, salty air, seafood-perfect whites.

Some vineyards are so steep that **grapes are harvested by monorail.** Liguria's Vermentino vines cling to sea cliffs so steep you can only harvest by hand—and often by rope.

Top Ligurian **wine producers** include Cantine Lunae Bosoni, Giacomelli, and Cheo, which are frequently awarded for their Vermentino and Sciacchetrà wines. Other highly-regarded producers are Terenzuola, Zangani, and Maccario Dringenberg for their Colli di Luni and Dolceacqua wines, respectively.

4

Central Italy

Tuscany

Famous For: Chianti, Brunello, Super Tuscans, rolling hills, cypress trees, and deep red romance.

The Chianti region was formally delimited in 1716 by the Grand Duke of Tuscany, the world's oldest protected wine zone.

Historic and Prestigious Estates in Tuscany:

Antinori: A prestigious and historic producer, known for pioneering the Super Tuscan movement with wines like Tignanello and Solaia.

Frescobaldi: Another historic family with roots dating to the 1300s, producing a wide range of wines, including Chianti and Brunello.

Tenuta San Guido: Producer of the acclaimed Super Tuscan, Sassicaia, which is often compared to fine Bordeaux wines.

Brunello di Montalcino specialists

Castello Banfi: A leading estate in Montalcino, known for modern winemaking and high-quality Brunello.

Biondi-Santi: Credited with inventing the Brunello di Montalcino in the 19th century, their wines are known for their longevity and elegance.

Ciacci Piccolomini d\'Aragona: Another highly-rated Brunello producer.

Umbria

Famous For: Sagrantino, Grechetto Big reds and honest whites with ancient roots.

Less touristy, more spiritual. Think vineyards + Etruscans.

Montefalco Sagrantino holds the record for the highest minimum aging requirement in Italy: four years (48 months in wood!).

Prominent producers:

Arnaldo Caprai: Arguably the most famous producer, this winery is credited with putting

Montefalco Sagrantino on the map by producing the first dry Sagrantino wines.

Tenuta Castelbuono: A highly-rated estate located in the communes of Bevagna and Montefalco.

Antonelli San Marco: A well-regarded winery situated in the heart of the Montefalco hills, known for its rich winemaking heritage.

Azienda Agricola Decugnano Dei Barbi: A "hidden gem" in Orvieto, combining ancient heritage with modern winemaking techniques.

Scacciadiavoli: A historic, family-run winery with a long history in the region.

Goretti: Frequently mentioned as a top winery for tours and tastings in Umbria.

Marche

Famous For: Verdicchio Clean, zippy whites with seaside vibes. A secret summer gem with oysters or olives.

Verdicchio's name comes from "verde" (green)—a nod to its vibrant acidity and the slightly green hue of its grapes.

Key wines and appellations to look for:

Verdicchio dei Castelli di Jesi DOCG: A highly-regarded white wine, with producers like Sartarelli and others receiving top awards.
Offida DOCG: Produces both Pecorino (white) and Rosso Passito (red), with Velenosi being a key producer.
Rosso Piceno DOC: A red wine from a blend of Montepulciano and Sangiovese grapes.
Lacrima di Morro d'Alba DOC: A unique aromatic red grape variety grown along the coast north of Ancona.
Vernaccia di Serrapetrona DOCG: A rare, high-alcohol, sparkling red wine made from the Vernaccia Nera grape. **Conero DOCG:** Produces full-bodied red wines primarily from Montepulciano grapes.

Lazio

Famous For: Frascati, the wine of emperors and trattorias. Light, refreshing, and practically made for pizza.
Frascati was dubbed "the wine of popes"—Papal palates from the Middle Ages onward favored this easy-drinking white.

Top wine producers in Lazio include well-known commercial estates like Casale del Giglio and the Famiglia Cotarella (formerly Falesco), as well as smaller, critically acclaimed producers such as Sergio Mottura, Tenuta di Fiorano, and Poggio Le Volpi. Other notable names are Cantina Costantini, Merumalia, and Damiano Ciolli.

Abruzzo

Famous For: Montepulciano d'Abruzzo Value-packed, juicy reds with bite.
Montepulciano d'Abruzzo grapes are often harvested by moonlight to preserve their delicate aromatics in the summer heat.

Renowned individual producers:

Emidio Pepe: A legendary, minimalist producer of age-worthy Montepulciano d'Abruzzo and Trebbiano d'Abruzzo wines.
Masciarelli Tenute Agricole: A large, quality-focused estate that remains influential despite the founder's passing.
Azienda Agricola Valentini: Famous for producing exceptional and long-lived Montepulciano d'Abruzzo and Trebbiano d'Abruzzo wines.
La Valentina: Produces top-quality Montepulciano d'Abruzzo, advised by the renowned enologist Luca D'Attoma.

5

Southern Italy

Campania

Famous For: Fiano, Greco di Tufo, Aglianico Grapes grown in Vesuvius' shadow = explosive character. Ancient Greek roots + modern finesse.

The volcanic soils of Mount Vesuvius give Campania's white Fiano and Greco di Tufo a signature smoky-mineral edge.

Top-tier producers:

Feudi di San Gregorio: A major producer in Campania, known for a range of wines, including Taurasi.

Mastroberardino: An iconic and historic winery with a strong reputation, particularly for Aglianico and Taurasi.

Galardi: A highly-regarded producer, noted for its influential wines.

Other highly-regarded producers:

Montevetrano: Known for its quality Aglianico-based wines.
Quintodecimo: A producer recognized for excellence in the region.
Marisa Cuomo: Celebrated for its white wines, especially from the Costa d'Amalfi region.
Villa Matilde: A well-respected producer, especially for Falerno del Massico.
Cantine Antonio Caggiano: A producer with a strong reputation, especially for Taurasi and Greco di Tufo.

Puglia

Famous For: Primitivo, Negroamaro, Juicy reds and rosés that party under olive trees.
Primitivo and Negroamaro vines here can live well over 100 years, earning them the nickname "grandfather vines."

Top wine producers in Puglia:

San Marzano: A well-known producer with many acclaimed wines.

Tenute Rubino: Known for being a pioneer in producing 100% Susumaniello wine and has significant vineyards around Brindisi.
Cantele: A notable producer in the Salento region, making both red and white wines.
Polvanera: Recognized for its role in the revival of Primitivo and Gioia del Colle wines.

Basilicata

Famous For: Aglianico del Vulture Bold, structured reds from volcanic soils.
Aglianico del Vulture hails from vines grown in old lava flows—some vineyards are planted in pits carved into volcanic rock!

Top wine producers in Basilicata include Cantine del Notaio, Elena Fucci, Carbone Vini, Cantine Re Manfredi, and Casa Vinicola D'Angelo. Other notable producers are Cantina del Vulture Vini, Cantine Balice, Cantine Taverna, and Basilisco.
These wineries are particularly recognized for their Aglianico del Vulture, a high-quality red wine from the region.

Calabria

Famous For: Gaglioppo, a red grape with aromas and flavors of sour cherry, wild herbs, dried rose, and tea-like tannin.
Backbone of Cirò.
Untamed landscapes, rugged wines.
Still off the radar = undiscovered treasures.

Notable wineries and producers:

Librandi: A historic and well-regarded estate, famous for its work with local grape varieties and its high-quality Cirò Rosso.
Cantine Benvenuto: Gained acclaim for its innovative Orange Zibibbo.
Ippolito 1845: A long-established winery.
Roberto Ceraudo: A pioneer of organic and biodynamic farming in the region, with wines like the Grisara Pecorello receiving awards.
Cantina Francesco Malena: A highly rated winery that is popular among visitors.
Antonella Lombardo: A producer recognized for its Greco wines.
Viola family: Known for their Moscato di Saracena, which has received top awards.

Molise

Famous For: Tintilia. Known for its deep color, low yields, and a distinctive profile of prunes, black pepper, and licorice, it produces full-bodied, aromatic wines.
Molise boasts ancient **Tintilia vines with roots dating to 1500 BCE**.

Notable producers:

Borgo di Colloredo: A third-generation family winery known for its commitment to sustainability and award-winning wines made from both native and international grapes.
Di Majo Norante: A historic and large-scale winery producing a range of wines, including those made from the Tintilia grape and a Metodo Classico Falanghina.
Campi Valerio: An estate in the Isernia province focused on showcasing the region's terroir with quality-driven wines.
Cantine Catabbo: A winery located in the province of Campobasso.
Tenute Martarosa: A family-owned winery situated near the village of Nuova Cliternia.

6

Italian Islands

Sicily

Famous For: Nero d'Avola, Grillo, Etna Rosso Volcanic slopes, ancient vineyards, and trendy natural wines. **Mount Etna's vineyards** sit at up to 1,000 m (3,300 ft), making them Europe's highest for growing red grapes like Nerello Mascalese.

Notable producers:

Planeta: A well-known and respected name in Sicilian winemaking, producing a wide range of wines.

Tasca d'Almerita: Another prominent producer, famous for its Tenuta Regaleali estate and wines like those made from Nero d'Avola.

Donnafugata: An award-winning winery known for its range of high-quality wines, including the renowned Ben Ryé passito.

Tenuta delle Terre Nere: A top producer in the Etna region, making elegant wines from Nerello Mascalese and Carricante grapes.

Other highly regarded wineries:

Frank Cornelissen: A producer from Etna known for natural wines.
Barone di Villagrande: An historic winery with a long tradition of winemaking in Sicily.
Benanti: An essential producer in the Etna region, credited with reviving the area's wine industry.

Sardinia

Famous For: Cannonau (Grenache), Vermentino Windswept, bold, and a little mysterious.
Cannonau (Grenache) is linked to Sardinia's famed centenarians—locals believe a glass a day keeps you living past 100!

Prominent producers to know:

Argiolas: A globally sought-after producer, particularly famous for its Turriga blend from Cannonau and Carignano grapes.

Sella & Mosca: A large and notable producer, independent of cooperatives, that makes a wide range of wines.

Cantina Santadi: A co-operative winery that produces highly rated wines, such as Terre Brune.

Agricola Punica: A producer that has gained acclaim for its high-quality Sardinian wines.

Cantina Mesa: Another well-regarded winery that produces wines from various Sardinian grape varieties.

Dettori Winery: A recognized producer, known for its wines that reflect the Sardinian terroir.

Cantina Oliena: A respected producer of Cannonau wines from the Barbagia region.

7

Italian Wine & Food Pairings by Region

One region, one wine, one iconic dish. Here are some hands-down favorites.

Valle d'Aosta
Wine: Petite Arvine
Pairing: Fontina cheese fondue (Fonduta Valdostana)
High-altitude freshness meets melty alpine comfort.

Piedmont (Piemonte)
Wine: Barolo (Nebbiolo)
Pairing: White truffle risotto
Elegant, earthy, luxurious—this is the haute couture of pairings.

Lombardy (Lombardia)
Wine: Franciacorta (sparkling)
Pairing: Veal Milanese
The bubbles cut the richness, balancing crisp with crunch.

Trentino-Alto Adige
Wine: Gewürztraminer
Pairing: Speck and apple slaw
Savory + sweet + aromatic = alpine harmony.

Veneto
Wine: Amarone della Valpolicella
Pairing: Pastissada de caval (slow-braised horse/beef stew)
Intensely flavored, just like the wine. Rustic and rich.

Friuli-Venezia Giulia
Wine: Friulano
Pairing: Frico (cheese and potato crisp)
Salty, crispy, golden goodness meets floral freshness.

Emilia-Romagna
Wine: Lambrusco (dry)
Pairing: Prosciutto di Parma + Parmigiano-Reggiano
Bubbly red + salty-sweet cured meats = aperitivo perfection.

Liguria
Wine: Vermentino

Pairing: Trofie al pesto Fresh basil, pine nuts, and sea breeze whites
Simple, sublime.

Tuscany (Toscana)
Wine: Chianti Classico
Pairing: Bistecca alla Fiorentina (Tuscan T-bone)
Structured red meets flame-grilled steak—power couple.

Umbria
Wine: Sagrantino di Montefalco
Pairing: Wild boar ragù
Dark, tannic, and bold—built for gamey, slow-cooked meat.

Marche
Wine: Verdicchio dei Castelli di Jesi
Pairing: Olive Ascolane (fried stuffed olives)
Zingy white + crispy snacks = Italian tapas moment.

Lazio
Wine: Frascati
Pairing: Spaghetti alla carbonara
Eggy richness lifted by a light, lemony white.

Abruzzo
Wine: Montepulciano d'Abruzzo
Pairing: Arrosticini (grilled lamb skewers)
Rustic red + charred meat = countryside picnic vibes.

Molise
Wine: Tintilia del Molise
Pairing: Cavatelli con ragù
Regional red with chewy, handmade pasta. Comfort food dreams.

Campania
Wine: Fiano di Avellino
Pairing: Spaghetti alle vongole (clams)
Mineral-rich white + briny seafood = pure Amalfi magic.

Basilicata
Wine: Aglianico del Vulture
Pairing: Caciocavallo cheese + grilled eggplant
Volcanic red meets smoky, salty, earthy flavors.

Puglia
Wine: Primitivo

Pairing: Orecchiette con cime di rapa (turnip greens)
Bold, ripe wine balanced by bitter greens + garlic kick.

Calabria
Wine: Gaglioppo
Pairing: 'Nduja on rustic bread
Spicy spread + rustic red = Southern Italian fire.

Sicily (Sicilia)
Wine: Nero d'Avola or Etna Rosso
Pairing: Caponata (sweet & sour eggplant)
Bright acidity + savory-sweet contrast.
Ancient flavors reborn.

Sardinia (Sardegna)
Wine: Vermentino di Gallura
Pairing: Bottarga spaghetti. Salty, citrusy, sea-kissed.
Like diving into the Med.

8

Italy Cheat Sheet

Wine Mood	Regions to Explore	Pairing Vibe
Crisp & coastal	Liguria, Campania, Sardinia	Seafood, herbs, lemon
Bold & meaty reds	Tuscany, Piedmont, Basilicata	Grilled or braised meats
Bubbly or fun	Lombardy, Emilia-Romagna, Veneto	Aperitivo, salty snacks, fried things
Aromatic whites	Trentino, Friuli, Marche	Cheese, veggies, pickled, or herbal
Off-the-beaten-path	Molise, Calabria, Umbria	Regional specialties & slow food

9

Italian Region Cheat Sheet

Style	Region
Light white?	Friuli, Liguria, Lazio
Big red?	Piedmont, Tuscany, Campania
Bubbly?	Veneto (Prosecco), Lombardy (Franciacorta)
Off-the-radar?	Molise, Basilicata, Marche
Volcanic & bold?	Sicily, Campania, Basilicata

10

Quick Recap

REDS-

Fun Fact: Tuscany = Chianti!
Chianti wines are predominantly made from the Sangiovese grape. While a minimum of 70% Sangiovese is required for Chianti, it can be blended with other approved red grape varieties, such as Canaiolo, Colorino, Cabernet Sauvignon, or Merlot.
Chianti Classico, a specific type of Chianti, must contain at least 80% Sangiovese.

This region is like the face of Italian wine. Chianti wine is a classic red wine, originating from this sunny, rolling region.
(Picture those beautiful vineyards!)
Visualize the Map: Italy is shaped like a boot, and its wine regions are scattered throughout.

The most famous ones are:

North: Piedmont (Barolo, Barbaresco) - big, bold reds
Central: Tuscany (Chianti, Brunello) - warm, fruity reds
South: Sicid'Avolao d'Avola) - strong, spicy reds Focus on the Faves:
Tuscany: Think of rolling hills, olive trees, and a glass of Chianti in your hand. It's one of the most popular regions.
Piedmont: Known for its rich Barolo wines. Deep flavors.
It's like Italian wine royalty.
Sicily: Warm weather makes for great wines. Think of sunny days and spicy reds.

If you enjoy fruity red wines, consider visiting Tuscany.
If you like bold, intense reds, head to Piedmont. Sicily is perfect for something spicy and Italian. Italy's wines are as varied as the country itself—like choosing between pasta shapes!

Italy isn't just about red wines — they've got some fantastic white wines too!

Italy is a land of diverse white wines, and they're delicious in their own right. These whites aren't just for sipping in the summer — they're perfect year-round!

The Famous White Wines:
Pinot Grigio (North, like in Veneto): Think of this as the light and crisp wine. It's like a refreshing breeze on a hot day.
Gavi (Piedmont): A bit more floral and elegant. It's a white wine with a little extra personality—a nice balance of fresh and crisp.
Verdicchio (Marche): A medium-bodied wine with hints of citrus and almond. It's like the perfect blend of fruity and nutty flavors!

Visualize the Regions:
North: Think cooler climate, where the white wines are light, crisp, and refreshing. Pinot Grigio and Gavi are the stars of the show.
Central: Regions like Marche and Lazio produce some beautifully balanced whites, such as Verdicchio and Frascati.
South: Even in the sunny, warm south, you'll find whites like Fiano and Greco di Tufo — slightly richer but still refreshing.

Fun Facts About White Wines:
Pinot Grigio is Italy's most famous white wine, loved for its easy-drinking style.
Fiano (from the South, like Campania) is like the "complex" white, with a bit of richness and minerality — think of it as the "wines for food lovers."
Frascati is the white wine of Rome! It's light, easy to drink, and perfect for summer.

If you want a light, fresh Italian wine, go for Pinot Grigio or Frascati. For something a bit floral and crisp, try Gavi. If you want something more complex, check out Fiano or Verdicchio!

11

France

Major Wine Regions of France

Copyright: The Society of Wine Educators 2022

12

Northern France

Champagne

Famous For: Champagne (obviously!)
Made mainly from Chardonnay, Pinot Noir, and Pinot Meunier. Cool climate = crisp acidity. That's why it bubbles with elegance.
Fun Fact: Only sparkling wine made in this region can legally be called "Champagne." The Champagne name is protected under international trade agreements, such as:
The Madrid Agreement and Lisbon Agreement (trademark protections), EU law, and bilateral treaties (like with the U.S., Australia, and others)

Large and popular producers

Moët & Chandon: The world's largest Champagne producer, known for its high volume.

Veuve Clicquot: A top seller in the U.S. market.
Nicolas Feuillatte: The best-selling Champagne in France.

13

Eastern France

Alsace

Famous For: Riesling, Gewürztraminer, and Pinot Gris. Bordering Germany, so it speaks both French and flavor fluently. Alsace Rieslings are almost always dry, unlike their German cousins. **Bonus:** The region boasts the highest number of organic and biodynamic producers in France, offering a diverse range of flavors, from floral to spicy.

Most celebrated producers:

Domaine Zind-Humbrecht
Founded in 1959, this biodynamic winery is run by Olivier Humbrecht, the first French Master of Wine. The family has been growing wine since 1620.
Wines: Specializes in concentrated, terroir-driven wines with intense flavor profiles.
Trimbach

Background: The Trimbach family has been producing wine in Ribeauvillé since 1626.
Wines: Widely considered a benchmark for classic Alsatian style, emphasizing structure and minerality over opulence.

Domaine Weinbach

Background: Founded by Capuchin monks in 1612, the estate was acquired by the Faller family in 1898. The winery has been practicing biodynamic viticulture since 2005.
Wines: Renowned for Rieslings, Gewürztraminers, and Pinot Gris. Their wines display a remarkable purity of aroma and incredible aging potential.

14

Central-Eastern France

Burgundy

Famous For: Pinot Noir (reds), Chardonnay (whites). Wines are subtle, refined, and often age-worthy.
Burgundy is **all about terroir**—some vineyard plots, (climats) are barely the size of a soccer field and have their own reputations.

Premier producers:

Domaine de la Romanée-Conti: Often referred to as "DRC," this estate is arguably the most famous and prestigious producer, known for its exclusive focus on Grand Cru wines.
Domaine Leroy: A legendary estate, also known as the "Queen of Burgundy" for its high-quality wines and powerful influence, according to Cult Wines and Rare Wine Invest.

Domaine Armand Rousseau: Another highly sought-after producer, famous for its Grand Cru Chambertin wine, according to Cult Wines and TasteAtlas.

Domaine Georges & Christophe Roumier: A highly-regarded producer, especially for its wines from Chambolle-Musigny.

15

South-Western France

Bordeaux

Famous For: Cabernet Sauvignon, Merlot, and Sauvignon Blanc.
Big, structured reds with lots of aging potential. Divided by rivers (**Left Bank, Right Bank**) and social drama (**Merlot vs. Cab**!).
The world's most famous wine blends were born here, and some Bordeaux vines are over 200 years old.
The **Left Bank is Cab-dominant**, the **Right Bank loves Merlot.** Want to age your wine 20 years? This is the region.
Tip: If you like serious, cellar-worthy reds or polished whites, Bordeaux is your royal court.

Some of **Bordeaux's top wine producers** include famous names like Château Lafite Rothschild, Château Latour, and Château Haut-Brion. Other highly regarded producers are Château Pétrus, Château Cheval Blanc, and Château Ausone. Many others are also recognized for their quality, with names like Château Ducru-Beaucaillou, Château Smith Haut Lafitte, and Château Pape Clément being frequently mentioned.

16

Southern France

Languedoc-Roussillon

Famous For: Blends — Grenache, Syrah, Carignan, Mourvèdre. Formerly the "jug wine" capital, it is now a hotspot for exciting, affordable bottles.

A vast, sunny region = a big variety and bold experimentation. Once known for bulk wine, Languedoc is now France's wildest region for innovation.

Organic farming? Natural wine? Indigenous grape revivals? It's all happening here, for less than $20 a bottle.

Think: Creative, rebellious wines that break the mold (and sometimes your budget in a good way).

Prominent producers:

Gérard Bertrand: A large, well-known producer with many wines across different appellations.
Mas de Daumas Gassac: A pioneering producer, particularly known for its red wines, even though it uses the IGP appellation rather than AOC for some of its top reds.
Domaine de la Rectorie: A producer in the Roussillon region, noted for its elegant and balanced wines that are influenced by the sea.
Domaine Danjou-Banessy: Considered a rising star in the Roussillon region.

17

South-Eastern France

Provence

Famous For: Rosé, baby!
Light, dry, salmon-pink wines are perfect for summer. **Grenache, Cinsault, Mourvèdre, Syrah** — all chilled to perfection. Rosé wasn't a trend here—it was a lifestyle long before Instagram.
Over 80% of the region's production is pink. Pair with lavender fields and fresh seafood.
Imagine: A seaside picnic with olives, lavender, and a bottle of rosé chilling in the Mediterranean breeze.

Popular and top-rated producers:

Château de Berne: A popular and highly rated winery known for its hotel, spa, and wine.
Château de la Gaude: Highly rated by visitors for tours and tastings.

Château Minuty: A well-known name in the region and the world.
Domaine Sainte Marie: A highly rated organic winery in the Côtes de Provence.
Other notable producers and estates:
Château La Coste: Known for its architecture and wine. **Domaines Bunan:** A respected organic producer in the Bandol appellation.
Château de Miraval: A notable producer with a wide range of wines.

18

Central France

Loire Valley

Famous For: Sauvignon Blanc (Sancerre), Chenin Blanc, and light reds like Cabernet Franc.

A long river, tons of castles, and a **whole lot of wine variety**. Zippy whites, floral sparklings, earthy reds — it's a tasting buffet. Known as the "Garden of France," the Loire has more white wine diversity than anywhere in the country—Sauvignon Blanc, Chenin Blanc, and Melon de Bourgogne all shine here. **Plus: castles. So many castles.**

If you like your wine crisp, fresh, and picnic-ready, Loire's your playground.

Top Loire Valley wine producers

include Ackerman (the largest producer in the region), Bouvet Ladubay (known for sparkling wine), and several highly regarded producers like Gérard Boulay, Henri Bourgeois, and

Didier Dagueneau, who are celebrated for their quality in specific appellations such as Sancerre and Pouilly-Fumé. Other notable producers are found across various appellations, such as Domaine Bernard Baudry in Chinon and Domaine de Bellivière in Jasnières.

19

South-Eastern France

Rhône Valley

Famous For: Syrah (North Rhône), Grenache-based blends (South Rhône). Think Hermitage, Côte-Rôtie, Châteauneuf-du-Pape. Spicy, powerful, and complex.
The Rhône is split into two distinct personalities: the north is characterized by all-Syrah and single-varietal intensity, while the South features Grenache blends and a sunny Mediterranean spice **(hello, Châteauneuf-du-Pape!)**
Best paired with: Roasted meats, fireplaces, and deep thoughts.

Northern Rhône:

E. Guigal: Considered one of the most consistent and comprehensive producers in the region, especially for its single-vineyard

Côte-Rôtie wines like La Landonne, La Turque, and La Mouline.

Chave: A historically significant and highly respected producer, particularly known for its Hermitage wines. Southern Rhône

Château de Beaucastel: One of the oldest and most famous estates.

Château Rayas: A historic and highly sought-after producer, considered a benchmark for Châteauneuf-du-Pape.

20

Quick Recap:

Wine Style	Go Here
Elegant Sparkling	Champagne
Aromatic Whites	Alsace
Earthy Reds & Refined Whites	Burgundy
Bold Reds & Cellar Gems	Bordeaux
Light Rosés & Relaxation	Provence
Crisp, Food- Loving Wines	Loire Valley
Spicy, Deep Reds	Rhône Valley
Creative, Bold Bottles	Languedoc

Choosing French Wine Is Like Booking a Vacation

Want sun and fun? Head to Provence, where the rosé flows like laughter on a terrace at golden hour. Think lavender fields, seafood platters, and bottles so pale they practically glow. These wines are your summer fling — crisp, easy, and Instagram-ready. **Want to impress a sommelier?** Whisper Burgundy and watch them nod in respect. This is where wine borders on religion. Pinot Noir and Chardonnay here are as expressive as French poetry — every slope, every soil nuance tells a story. Be prepared to spend more, but you'll earn bragging rights and possibly a spiritual awakening.

Feeling bold and brooding? Pack your emotional baggage and head to Bordeaux. This is where Cabernet Sauvignon and Merlot get serious — structured, powerful, and age-worthy. Bordeaux is a tuxedoed dinner party where everyone's debating philosophy and nobody's leaving early.

Need wine with your cheese board? Say bonjour to Loire and Alsace. Loire gives you refreshing Sauvignon Blancs and soft reds like Chinon — perfect for goat cheese or lazy picnics by the river. Alsace, meanwhile, is the aromatic escape — Riesling, Gewürztraminer, and Pinot Gris bursting with spice and charm. These wines flirt with sweetness but keep it classy.

Want to explore on a budget? Languedoc is your hidden gem — wild, sun-soaked, and unpretentious. Here, the wines are generous, the prices are friendly, and the locals are too busy enjoying life to care about scores or status. Expect Grenache, Syrah, and Carignan with Mediterranean swagger.

21

French Food & Wine Pairings

Champagne

Food: Oysters, caviar, triple-cream cheese (Brillat-Savarin!), gougères.
Pair with: Brut Champagne
High acidity + bubbles = cuts through richness like a sabre. Rosé Champagne works with duck rillettes or smoked salmon.

Alsace

Food: Choucroute garnie (sauerkraut + sausages), Munster cheese, tarte flambée.
Pair with: Riesling (dry) or Gewürztraminer.
Aromatic whites = perfect with spiced or fermented foods. Try Pinot Gris with foie gras for a full sensory "ooh-la-la."

Burgundy

Food: Coq au vin, beef bourguignon, escargots, and epoisses cheese.
Pair with:
Pinot Noir (for earthy, savory dishes)
Chardonnay (esp. Meursault or Chablis with creamy sauces)
If it's swimming in butter or wine, Burgundy's got a wine for it.

Bordeaux

Food: Entrecôte à la Bordelaise (ribeye in red wine sauce), lamb, duck confit.
Pair with: Left Bank Red Bordeaux (Cabernet-led) for grilled meats Right Bank (Merlot-led) for stews and mushrooms.
Bordeaux Blanc (a blend of Sauvignon Blanc and Sémillon) works magic with shellfish.

Loire Valley

Food: Goat cheese (Crottin de Chavignol), fish in beurre blanc, rillettes.
Pair with:

Sancerre / Pouilly-Fumé (Sauvignon Blanc) for crisp, grassy pairings. Vouvray (Chenin Blanc) with roast poultry or pork.
Cabernet Franc reds = dreamy with charcuterie.

Provence

Food: Bouillabaisse, ratatouille, tapenade, Niçoise salad.
Pair with: Dry Rosé from Provence
Refreshing, herbal, and a match for tomatoes and olive oil.
If you're grilling seafood or dining seaside, rosé is your wingman.

Rhône Valley

Food: Lamb with herbs, duck breast, lentil stew, cassoulet.
Pair with:
Northern Rhône (Syrah) – peppery and bold, for game or grilled meat.
Southern Rhône (Grenache blends) – Châteauneuf-du-Pape with cassoulet.
Spice + Syrah = culinary seduction.

Languedoc & Roussillon

Food: Grilled lamb with garlic, cassoulet, wild boar stew.
Pair with: Robust red blends (Grenache, Mourvèdre, Syrah) Rustic food, bold wine. These are the rebels of the French table. Great for BBQ, sausages, and bold cheeses.

BONUS ROUND: Cheese + Wine Combos

Cheese	Wine Pairing
Brie or Camembert	Champagne or light Burgundy
Roquefort (blue)	Sauternes (sweet wine)
Goat cheese	Sancerre (Loire)
Comté	Vin Jaune (Jura) or Chardonnay
Époisses (funky, stinky)	Red Burgundy

22

Greece

Main Wine Regions of Greece

23

Northern Greece – Macedonia & Thrace

Naoussa (Macedonia)

Famous For: Xinomavro
Think: Sour cherries, sun-dried tomatoes, iron, and firm tannins. Often compared to **Nebbiolo** for its age-worthiness and elegance, Xinomavro means "acid black"—and it delivers.
Fun Fact: Naoussa became the first Greek wine region to earn PDO status in 1971. Xinomavro can age gracefully for decades in this region.

Major producers:

Tikveš Winery: The oldest and largest winery in North Macedonia, founded in 1885, and considered one of the most important on the Balkan Peninsula.

Ezimit Vino: A successful winery that consistently ranks among the largest and most profitable in North Macedonia.
Other notable wineries:
Stobi Winery: A modern winery near the ancient town of Stobi, cultivating vineyards on 13,000 hectares and known for its Vranec wine.
Bovin Winery: The first family winery in North Macedonia, established in 1998, and is a significant exporter of its wines.
Kamnik Winery: Located in the Skopje wine region, this winery is known for producing world-class wines.

Drama & Amyndeon

Famous For: Assyrtiko (inland!), Sauvignon Blanc, Cabernet blends
Think: Crisp altitude whites, structured reds, alpine freshness. Amyndeon is the highest-altitude PDO in Greece, producing light, cool-climate Xinomavro and even some rosé bubbles.

Prominent Amyndeon wine producers

Alpha Estate: Founded in 1997 by viticulturist Makis Mavridis and oenologist Angelos Iatridis, it is considered one of

Greece's most cutting-edge wineries and is recognized for its high-altitude vineyards.
Ktima Kir-Yianni: This winery, founded by Yiannis Boutaris, has a second winery in Amyndeon that focuses on the local Xinomavro grape, producing traditional-method sparkling rosés and other styles.
Domaine Karanika: This winery uses a network of organic vineyards across seven different villages in the Amyndeon appellation to create wines that express the distinct characteristics of each terroir.
Paranga Winery: A winery located in the Amyndeon region with 30 hectares of privately owned vineyards.
Boutari: This large Greek winery works in multiple regions, including Amyndeon, producing both tank-method and more complex sparkling wines.

24

Central Greece – Thessaly & Sterea Ellada

Rapsani (Mount Olympus)

Famous For: Xinomavro, Krassato, Stavroto blends
Think: Earthy, spicy, medium-bodied reds with a mythic mood. Grown on the slopes of Mount Olympus, these wines are the drink of gods—literally.
Fun Fact: Rapsani is one of the few PDOs that requires a blend of indigenous reds rather than single varietals.

Top producers of Rapsani wine, which is from the Rapsani PDO on the slopes of Mount Olympus in Greece, include Tsantali and Thymiopoulos Vineyards. The wine is a blend of the indigenous Greek grapes Xinomavro, Krassato, and Stavroto.

Central Greece IGP (Sterea Ellada)

Famous For: Malagousia
Think: White peach, jasmine, and a soft floral touch.
Malagousia was nearly extinct until it was revived in the 1970s. Now it's a darling of sommeliers around the world.

Top wine producers in Sterea Ellada (Central Greece) include established wineries like Papagiannakos, Avantis, and Hatzimichalis, known for their work with both indigenous and international varieties. Greek Wine Cellars D. Kourtakis is a major producer with a significant presence in the region, operating wineries in locations like Ritsona. The region is a diverse wine-producing area, home to varieties such as Savatiano, Roditis, and the rare red Mouchtaro grape.

Top producers of Malagousia wine in Sterea Ellada include Ktima Kir-Yianni and Alpha Estate. At the same time, other notable wineries producing Malagousia in the broader region are Domaine Gerovassiliou and Domaine Skouras.

25

North-West Greece

Epirus

Famous For: Debina
Think: Zippy, slightly sparkling whites with a hint of lemon zest. One of the coolest, wettest regions in Greece—perfect for crisp mountain wines and pét-nat-style fizz.
Fun Fact: Debina wines from Zitsa often come with a natural spritz, and the area is known for traditional semi-sparkling production.

Leading wineries

Katogi Averoff: A well-known estate in Metsovo that combines wine, art, and hospitality. They cultivate both international varieties like Cabernet Sauvignon and indigenous ones like Vlachiko.

Zoinos Winery: A producer that focuses on the native Debina grape, which is used to make unique sparkling wines.
Domaine Glinavos: A winery with vineyards in the mountainous forests of Epirus, contributing to the region's wine production.
Key wine regions and their producers
PGI Metsovo: This region is located on the southeastern tip of Ioannina and features vineyards at high altitudes. Producers here work with grapes such as Debina, Vlahiko, Cabernet Sauvignon, and Gewurztraminer.
PDO Zitsa: Located on the western slopes of the Pindos range, this region's regulations permit only the native Debina grape.

26

Peloponnese – The Greek Southern Mainland

Nemea (Corinthia)

Famous For: Agiorgitiko
Think: Juicy plum, baking spice, velvety texture.
Agiorgitiko is known as the "Blood of Hercules."
Smooth but age-worthy, it's Greece's most planted red grape
Fun Fact: Nemea is home to Greece's most extensive red wine PDO and has altitudes ranging from sea level to 900+ meters.

Top Nemea wine producers

Domain Skouras: A highly recognized and respected winery in the region.
Papaioannou Winery: A historic, family-run business known for its high-quality, organic wines and extensive vineyards.

Ktima Palivou: This winery produces wines of excellent quality, often blending Agiorgitiko with French varietals.
Ktima Tselepos: Listed as one of the most popular wineries to visit in Nemea.
Aivalis Winery: Known for a wide range of wines, including premium and single-vineyard selections made from Agiorgitiko and blends.
Estate Constantin Gofas: A winery recognized for excellent wines, reasonable prices, and friendly staff.

Mantinia (Arcadia)

Famous For: Moschofilero
Think: Rose petals, grapefruit, and cool-climate zip.
A pink-skinned white grape that makes aromatic whites with attitude. Great for summer sipping.
Fun Fact: Mantinia is located at a high elevation (~650m), which helps preserve the acidity in Moschofilero even in the hot Mediterranean summers.

Key producers in Arcadia

Ktima Tselepos: A renowned family-owned winery focused on Moschofilero and other indigenous grapes, with a focus on quality and the unique terroir of Arcadia.
Troupis Winery: A popular winery with a tasting room and atmospheric outdoor areas, located just outside of Tripoli.
Ktima Spiropoulos: A winery that was among the first to bring Moschofilero to the forefront of the Greek wine scene.
Bosinakis Winery: Known for producing excellent examples of white Moschofilero, including from the PDO Mantinia appellation.
Domaine Skouras: While not solely based in Arcadia, this producer has a significant presence in the broader Peloponnese region and is known for its elegant wines.

27

Greek Islands – Aegean & Ionian

Santorini (Cyclades)

Famous For: Assyrtiko
Think: Sea salt, lemon rind, volcanic smoke. These ancient, basket-trained vines (called kouloura) produce some of the most mineral-driven white wines in the world.
Fun Fact: Some Assyrtiko vines are over 200 years old, grown on ungrafted rootstock in volcanic soils—phylloxera never made it here.

Top Santorini wine producers include Estate Argyros, Santo Wines, Domaine Sigalas, and Hatzidakis Winery, with others like Gaia Winery, Vassaltis Vineyards, and Venetsanos Winery also frequently mentioned. These wineries are known for their high-quality wines, especially those made from the native Assyrtiko grape, and often highlight the island's unique volcanic terroir.

Crete (Heraklion & Lasithi)

Famous For: Vidiano, Liatiko, Kotsifali
Think: Herbs, stone fruit, sun-warmed red berries. Crete is one of the oldest wine regions in the world—the Minoans were fermenting wine here over 4,000 years ago. **Fun Fact:** The island's archaeological sites include wine presses from 1,600 BCE.
Crete = ancient terroir with a modern twist.

Prominent producers:

Lyrarakis Winery: Celebrated for reviving rare indigenous grapes like Plyto and Dafni.
Manousakis Winery: Known for organic practices and full-bodied wines, often using varieties like Syrah and Roussanne.
Douloufakis Winery: A historic winery that blends tradition with modern techniques.
Dourakis Winery: A family-owned estate in Chania, known for its restored buildings and handcrafted wines. **Alexakis S.A. - Alexakis Winery:** A large winery that focuses on indigenous varieties but also produces international blends.
Karavitakis Winery: Recognized for being one of the first to produce high-quality Vidiano.
Domaine Paterianakis: An organic, boutique winery located in the hills south of Heraklion.

Samos (Northeast Aegean)

Famous For: Muscat Blanc à Petits Grains
Think: Apricot jam, orange blossom, sweet spice.

Samos is renowned for its dessert wines—some of which rival Tokaji and Sauternes in richness and balance.

Fun Fact: The Muscat vines here hug steep terraces and benefit from marine winds that keep them fresh, even when sweet.

Leading wine producers:

United Winemaking Agricultural Cooperative of Samos (UWC Samos): Founded in 1934, this is the largest and one of the oldest cooperatives in Greece. It represents a vast number of local vine growers and is a major exporter of Samos wines. The cooperative operates two modern wineries and is known for producing a wide range of wines, including popular styles like Samos Vin Doux, Gran Cru, and Nectar.

Kostaki Winery: Established in 2023, this newer winery focuses on modern, high-quality wines from the Muscat à Petits Grains variety.

Hatziioannou Organic Winery: This winery is dedicated to organic farming and uses traditional techniques to produce wines from the Muscat White Mikrorogo variety.

Vakakis Wines: Founded in 2011, this producer focuses on crafting a limited number of high-quality wines, highlighting local treasures.

Nopera Winery: With roots tracing back to the 19th century, this was the first private winery on Samos to open after a change in legislation in 2013.

Paros, Tinos, Rhodes & Beyond

Famous For: Mandilaria, Monemvasia, Aidani

Think: Salty reds, exotic whites, and experimental blends.

Each island has its micro-PDO, native grapes, and microclimate. It's like a grape safari across the Aegean.

Fun Fact: Some vines on islands like Tinos and Paros are grown without trellising, crawling low along the ground to survive high winds.

28

Cheat Sheet –Wine Vibes Across Greece

Style	Region	Native Grape(s)
Powerful, structured red	Naoussa, Nemea	Xinomavro, Agiorgitiko
Mineral, salty white	Santorini, Drama	Assyrtiko
Aromatic, floral white	Mantinia, Central Greece	Moschofilero, Malagousia
Sweet + luxurious white	Samos	Muscat Blanc
Sparkling or spritzy	Epirus (Zitsa)	Debina
Island herbal & bold	Crete, Paros	Vidiano, Liatiko, Mandilar

29

Greek Food & Wine Pairings by Region

Northern Greece – Macedonia & Thrace Naoussa (Xinomavro)

Wine: Xinomavro – high-acid, tannic, tomato-y red
Pairing: Lamb giouvetsi (slow-braised lamb with tomato & orzo). Why it works: The wine's acidity matches the tomato base, and the tannins stand up to lamb.

Amyndeon / Florina (Xinomavro, Sparkling Rosé)

Wine: Xinomavro Rosé or sparkling dry reds
Pairing: Bougiourdi (baked feta with peppers & tomato).
Why it works: Zippy acidity + salty cheese = magic.

Drama / Kavala (Assyrtiko, Sauvignon Blanc blends)

Wine: Crisp white blends
Pairing: Grilled sea bass with lemon & herbs.
Why it works: Minerality mirrors the fish's lightness and fresh lemon zest.

Central Greece – Thessaly & Sterea Ellada Rapsani (Xinomavro blends)

Wine: Xinomavro, Krassato, Stavroto blend
Pairing: Roast wild boar or pork with herbs.
Why it works: The earthy blend pairs well with gamey, woodsy meats.

Sterea Ellada (Malagousia)

Wine: Malagousia – floral, lush white
Pairing: Grilled zucchini or squash blossoms with feta.
Why it works: Elegant aromatics lift the creamy, vegetal flavors.

Epirus (Debina – Zitsa)

Wine: Debina – light, fresh, sometimes sparkling
Pairing: Grilled trout with lemon and herbs.

Why it works: The wine's bright profile mirrors mountain stream freshness.

Peloponnese Nemea (Agiorgitiko)

Wine: Agiorgitiko – plush, spicy, soft tannins
Pairing: Moussaka (eggplant, meat, béchamel)
Why it works: The combination of round tannins and baking spice creates a cozy harmony with the layers of moussaka.

Mantinia (Moschofilero)

Wine: Moschofilero – floral, citrusy white
Pairing: Shrimp saganaki (feta, tomato, ouzo)
Why it works: Floral and citrus notes cut through the richness and complement the bright sauce.

Greek Islands
Santorini (Assyrtiko)

Wine: Assyrtiko – saline, citrus, volcanic
Pairing: Octopus grilled with olive oil and oregano.
Why it works: The wine's minerality echoes the sea-salt-kissed flavors.

Crete (Vidiano, Liatiko, Kotsifali)

Wine: Vidiano (white): peachy, herbal Liatiko (red): light, spicy
Pairing: Dakos salad (barley rusk, tomato, mizithra cheese) with Vidiano Cretan lamb with rosemary for Liatik.
Why it works: Local herbs and slow-roasting mirror the gentle strength of these wines.

Samos (Muscat Blanc – dessert wine)

Wine: Samos Vin Doux – sweet, rich Muscat
Pairing: Baklava or cheese + honey
Why it works: Sweet on sweet = indulgence, but acidity keeps it balanced.

Paros, Tinos, Cycladic Islands (Mandilaria, Monemvasia, Aidani)

Wine: Aidani (white): soft, floral Mandilaria (red): tannic, rustic
Pairing: Fried calamari with lemon for Aidani, Goat stew with wild greens for Mandilaria
Why it works: Local ingredients meet their match in these bold, regional wines.

30

Pairing Guide

Region	Grape	Dish
Naoussa	Xinomavro	Braised lamb with tomato
Amyndeon	Sparkling Rosé	Baked feta with tomato + chili
Rapsani	Xinomavro blend	Wild boar or herbed pork
Sterea Ellada	Malagousia	Stuffed zucchini blossoms
Epirus(Zitsa)	Debina	Grilled trout

Region	Grape	Dish
Nemea	Agiorgitiko	Moussaka or pastitsio
Mantinia	Moschofiler	Shrimp saganaki
Santorini	Assyrtiko	Grilled octopus
Crete	Vidiano/Liatiko	Dakos salad / Slow-roasted lamb
Samos	Muscat	Baklava or sweet cheese + honey

31

Spain

Major Wine Regions of Spain

32

Northern Spain

Rioja

Famous For: Tempranillo-based reds (Reserva & Gran Reserva)
Think: Dusty bookshelves, leather chairs, and cherry-scented nostalgia.
This is Spain's most iconic wine region. Aging is everything here— Gran Reservas can rest for a decade before release.
Rioja wines are aged in oak barrels to such an extent that they have developed their own classification system: Crianza, Reserva, and Gran Reserva. Tempranillo here is like Spain's answer to Pinot Noir and Cabernet—elegant but with swagger.
Fun Fact: Rioja was the first region in Spain to earn DOC status
(Denominación de Origen Calificada), Spain's highest wine honor.

Traditional and historic producers:

La Rioja Alta: A producer known for its commitment to tradition and elegant, classic styles.

López de Heredia: An iconic and historic producer that ages its wines longer than the required period for their classifications.

Marqués de Murrieta: A revered and historic producer, with wines like the Castillo Ygay Gran Reserva Especial receiving high acclaim.

Modern and boutique producers

Beronia: A producer recognized for sustainable winemaking practices.

Ramón Bilbao: A producer known for innovation in Rioja. CVNE (Compañía Vinícola del Norte de España): A famous producer with a long history in Rioja.

Ribera del Duero

Famous For: Powerful, inky reds from Tempranillo (locally called Tinto Fino)
Think: Bold flavors, high elevation, and big structure.
The secret? Altitude. These wines are grown at high elevations, where intense days and chilly nights combine to create slow-ripening magic. Vega Sicilia, Spain's most legendary wine, hails from here. Bordeaux meets brawn. If Rioja is velvet, Ribera is leather.
Fun Fact: Vega Sicilia, Spain's most legendary wine estate, is here—and yes, bottles can go for thousands.

Established and legendary producers:

Vega Sicilia: A historic and prestigious winery known for its Unico Gran Reserva.
Dominio de Pingus: A cult winery famous for its high-end "Pingus" wine, made by Peter Sisseck.
Pesquera: A classic producer founded in 1972, known for wines like the Tinto Pesquera Crianza.
Modern and highly acclaimed producers

Aalto: Considered a top modern producer in the region.
Pago de Carraovejas: A popular and highly regarded winery that has grown significantly since the 1970s.
Dominio de Atauta: Another producer frequently mentioned for its quality and acclaim.

Bierzo

Famous For: Mencía (floral, medium-bodied reds) **Think:** Pinot Noir's Spanish cousin, but with a bit more spice and sass.
Tucked in northwest Spain, Bierzo is all about old vines, steep vineyards, and a "cool climate" edge.

Leading producers:

Descendientes de J. Palacios: A partnership between Álvaro Palacios and his nephew Ricardo Pérez Palacios, this winery focuses on old-vine Mencía grapes from steep hillsides, producing iconic wines like Pétalos del Bierzo, Las Lamas, and La Faraona.

Raúl Pérez Viticultor: An influential winemaker in the region, who has been involved with several estates, including his family's Bodegas Castro Ventosa. He is known for wines like Ultreia de Valtuille.

Casar de Burbia: Produces highly-regarded wines such as Tebaida and Casar de Burbia.

Estefanía: Known for its Tilenus range of wines, including Tilenus Envejecido en Roble and Tilenus Pagos de Posada.

Godelia: A prominent producer of both red and white wines, with notable wines like Godelia white Sobre Lías and Godelia 12 Meses Roble.

Bodegas Castro Ventosa: The family winery where Raúl Pérez had his start, it produces wines such as El Castro de Valtuille and Valtuille Cepas Centenarias.

Rías Baixas (Galicia)

Famous For: Albariño
Think: Seaspray, citrus, and fresh oysters. Albariño is the queen of Atlantic whites—zippy, aromatic, and made for seafood.
Fun Fact: Many vines are trained on pergolas to avoid damp soil and allow airflow in the rainy Galician climate.

Top wine producers in Rías Baixas include large cooperatives and smaller, quality-focused wineries, such as Bodegas Martín Códax, Pazo de Señorans, Zárate, Palacio de Fefiñanes, and Pazo de Barrantes. These producers are known for high-quality Albariño wines, with some focusing on traditional methods and others on modern techniques to express the unique terroir of the region.

33

Eastern Spain

Catalonia (Catalunya)

Famous For: Cava (Spain's answer to Champagne), Priorat reds
Think: Sparkles, slate soils, and bold experimentation.
Cava uses the traditional method (like Champagne) with native grapes like Macabeo and Xarel·lo.
Priorat = bold reds from slate-laced mountains, powered by Garnacha & Cariñena.
Fun Fact: Cava producers are breaking away from the "cheap and cheerful" stereotype with single-village crus and serious aging.

Some of Catalonia's top wine producers include Bodegas Torres (a large, well-known producer) and Gramona, Alta Alella, and Recaredo, which are highly regarded for their Cava. Other top producers known for specific styles or regions include Raimat (in Costers del Segre), Celler Pardas and Enric Soler (known for still Xarel·lo), and various wineries in the Priorat region like Bodega Atavus Priorat and Bodega Celler Mas Doix.

Valencia & Alicante

Famous For: Monastrell (aka Mourvèdre)
Think: Warm, ripe, and a little wild.
These regions are hot, coastal, and full of value—perfect for bold Mediterranean reds and dry, salty whites.
The Valencia Designation of Origin (DO) is a diverse wine region with different subzones and a mix of traditional and modern winemakers.

Notable producers include:

Celler del Roure: Celebrated for its unique approach to winemaking, which involves aging wine in historic subterranean caves and prioritizing local grape varieties like Mandó and Monastrell.
Bodegas Hispano Suizas: This winery in the Utiel-Requena DO (within the greater Valencia region) is known for its high-end wines, including the premium Pinot Noir,

Bassus, and the excellent sparkling Tantum Ergo.

Bodegas Enguera: A pioneer in organic and sustainable viticulture, this producer creates a range of quality red and white wines, including fresh rosés.

Mustiguillo: A leader in the Utiel-Requena region, this estate is known for its focus on the native Bobal grape and is recognized with its own Pago certification, a high-quality classification.

Top Alicante wine producers:

The Alicante DO is particularly famous for its robust red wines made from the Monastrell grape, as well as its historic Fondillón sweet wine. Leading wineries in the region include:

Enrique Mendoza: A highly respected producer that has elevated the quality of Alicante wines. They are known for their Monastrell- based reds and use of international varieties like Cabernet Sauvignon and Merlot.

Casa Agrícola Pepe Mendoza: With vineyards in the Pla de Lliber, this winery focuses on crafting high-quality wines that express the region's unique climate and soil.

They are highly regarded for their dedication to quality.

34

Central Spain

Castilla-La Mancha

Famous For: Airén (world's most planted white grape), plus Tempranillo & Garnacha
Think: Wide skies, windmills, and wine at scale.
This is Spain's engine room—the largest wine-producing region in the world by land. But it's not just bulk anymore: organic, high-altitude, and **old-vine reds** are turning heads.

Premium, Single-Estate and Boutique Wineries:

Dominio de Valdepusa: Awarded the first DO Pago designation in Spain, this estate is known for high- quality wines from international grape varieties like Syrah, Petit Verdot, and Cabernet Sauvignon.

Bodegas Verum: A family-run winery in Tomelloso that focuses on organic and biodynamic wines.
Bodegas Hacienda Villarta: Known for producing fine wines in the Toledo area.
Bodegas Gratias. Familia Y Viñedos: An artisanal, family-owned winery that works with nearly extinct indigenous grape varieties.
Large Cooperatives and Value Producers:
Bodegas Campos Reales: A cooperative that produces high-quality wines at accessible prices. **Vinicola De Tomelloso:** A winery with medieval caves and a pump house.

Madrid

Famous For: Garnacha
Think: City skyline meets ancient vines.
Just outside the capital, Madrid's high-elevation vineyards are producing bright, spicy Garnacha—easy to drink, hard to forget.

Top wineries in the Vinos de Madrid DO:

Bodega Marañones:
Marañones is a leader in producing high-quality wines in the Sierra de Gredos area, and

it has become a benchmark for the Vinos de Madrid DO.

The winery was founded by Fernando García and Fernando Cornejo.

It is particularly known for its expressive Garnacha wines.

Comando G:

Located in the Sierra de Gredos mountains west of Madrid, Comando G is highly regarded for its unique, high-elevation wines.

The winery focuses on producing exceptional Garnacha from old vines.

It is not always open for visitors, so contacting them in advance is recommended.

35

Southern Spain

Jerez (Sherry Country)

Famous For: Sherry (from bone-dry Fino to sweet Pedro Ximénez). It's made from three white grapes: **Palomino**, the most common, used for most dry styles; **Pedro Ximénez** (PX), used for sweet sherry; and **Moscatel**, also used for sweet wines.
Think: Nutty, salty, complex—wine's misunderstood genius. Sherry isn't just your grandma's after-dinner drink—
It's layered, aged under flor yeast, and unique.
Fun Fact: Aged in solera* systems, where new wine blends with old, like liquid time travel.

Prominent producers:

Bodegas Lustau: Known for high-quality sherry and is well- regarded for its guided tours and historic cellars.

Bodegas Fundador: One of the oldest wineries in Spain, dating back to 1730, and a producer of both brandy and sherry.
Bodegas Valdespino: Considered one of the oldest, with a history dating back to the 13th century.

*The Solera system is a fractional blending and aging method, originating in the Jerez region, where liquid is continuously aged in a pyramid of barrels with the oldest at the bottom and the newest at the top. When a portion of the oldest liquid (the "solera") is drawn for bottling, it's replaced with wine from the next oldest layer (the "first criadera"), which is then topped up with liquid from the layer above it, and so on. This process ensures consistency and maintains complexity by gradually aging and blending liquids over time.

Montilla-Moriles

Famous For: Pedro Ximénez (PX)
Think: Sun-dried grapes, unctuous sweetness, and amber-hued elegance.

This region makes Sherry-style wines but doesn't legally call them "Sherry." It's drier, hotter, and pure PX territory.

Major producers:

Alvear: As the oldest winery in Andalusia, founded in 1729, Alvear is a benchmark for quality in the region. It produces a wide range of wines, including dry and sweet wines, and is known for its excellent PX wines and for reintroducing single-harvest wines.
Toro Albalá: Founded in 1922, this winery is famous for its impressive collection and production of vintage PX wines.
Pérez Barquero: A historic winery founded in 1905, it is a significant producer in the region and is often sought out by independent bottlers like Equipo Navazos.

36

Islands of Spain

Canary Islands (Islas Canarias)

Famous For: Listán Negro & Listán Blanco
Think: Lava, altitude, and ancient ungrafted vines.
Wines here are grown on volcanic ash, often trained in crater-like hollows to protect from the wind.
Fun Fact: These vines are phylloxera-free—like stepping back in time.

Canary Islands Wine Producers:

Bodegas El Grifo: Founded in 1775, this is the oldest winery in the Canary Islands and is located on Lanzarote.
Bodegas Viñátigo: A family winery located on Tenerife that focuses on sustainable winemaking.

Bodegas Los Bermejos: Another Lanzarote winery that is known for its high-quality wines.
Bodegas Teneguía: A cooperative winery on La Palma with over 280 members that blends traditional methods with modern techniques.
Bodegas Monje: Situated in the Tacoronte-Acentejo region of Tenerife, this winery is known for its stunning views of Mount Teide.

Balearic Islands (Mallorca, Menorca)

Famous For: Callet & Manto Negro
Think: Beach wine with heritage.
The islands are embracing native grapes and reviving nearly lost varieties with gorgeous Mediterranean flair.

Historic wineries:

Bodega Ribas: The oldest winery on the island, with over 300 years of history.
Bodegas Macià Batle: Established in 1856 and located near Santa María del Camí, it is known for its innovative and artistic wine labels and award-winning wines.
Modern and boutique wineries
Bodegas Ànima Negra: A younger vineyard founded in 1994 near Felanitx.
Son Prim: A smaller winery in Sencelles that specializes in powerful, oak-aged red wines.
Vins Miquel Gelabert: An artisan winemaker in Manacor known for his experimental approach and variety of wines.

37

Spanish Food & Wine Pairing Guide

Rioja (Tempranillo-based Reds)

Food: Jamón ibérico, grilled lamb chops, Manchego cheese, chorizo.
Pair with: Crianza or Reserva Rioja Why it works: Tempranillo's earthy red fruit + balanced oak = perfect with salty, savory meats.
Bonus: A Gran Reserva is your match for slow-roasted pork or mushroom paella.

Rías Baixas (Albariño)

Food: Oysters, octopus (pulpo a la gallega), seafood paella, lemony ceviche.
Pair with: Zesty, mineral Albariño Why it works: High acid + salinity + citrus = seafood's best friend.
Think: A squeeze of lemon but make it wine.

Ribera Del Duero (Tinto Fino / Tempranillo)

Food: Grilled steak, morcilla (blood sausage), roasted eggplant, aged cheeses.
Pair with: Bold Ribera reds
Why it works: Intense reds pair well with umami and char. Altitude-grown grapes keep it fresh.
Pro tip: Decant it and serve with anything grilled over an open flame.
Sherry (Jerez)
Fino/Manzanilla: Marcona almonds, olives, sushi, anchovies
Amontillado: Jamón, roasted mushrooms, nutty cheeses
PX (Pedro Ximénez): Blue cheese, figs, chocolate desserts Why it works: Sherry's got layers—and a wine for every course.
Note: Fino is bone dry. PX is syrup-sweet. Treat them like an entire menu.

Priorat (Garnacha & Cariñena blends)

Food: Game meats, wild mushroom dishes, lamb stew, aged Manchego
Pair with: Intense, mineral-rich Priorat Why it works: Slate soils = structured, brooding wines that need bold, earthy food.

Think: Wild flavors + mountain wine.

Valencia / Alicante (Monastrell)

Food: Spicy sausages, grilled eggplant, lamb burgers, paprika-rich stews
Pair with: Monastrell (Mourvèdre)
Why it works: Ripe fruit + tannin + spice = total harmony. **Fun fact:** Monastrell is known to pair well with smoky or charred foods.

Catalonia (Cava, Priorat, etc.)

Food: Tapas galore—garlic shrimp, patatas bravas, croquetas
Pair with:
Cava Brut: Fried or salty snacks
Rosé Cava: Charcuterie, grilled vegetables
Priorat: Lamb or mushroom paella Why it works: Bubbles + acid = cuts through decadent bites. Priorat = power and precision.

Canary Islands (Listán Negro & Blanco)

Food: Grilled fish, goat cheese, mojo rojo sauces, smoky potatoes
Pair with: Volcanic whites or lightly smoky reds

Why it works: Wines from ash-rich soils have a natural saltiness and smokiness, making them an ideal pairing with coastal fare.

Montilla-Moriles (Pedro Ximénez)

Food: Chocolate cake, flan, blue cheese with honey, dried figs
Pair with: Sweet PX
Why it works: It's like pouring caramel on your dessert plate— but balanced with acidity. Also great as a drizzle over vanilla ice cream.

38

Quick Recap: Spain's Wine Regions by Style

Wine Style	Go Here
Classic, Age-Worthy Reds	Rioja
Elegant Sparkling	Catalonia (Cava)
Crisp, Salty Whites	Rías Baixas (Albariño)
Bold Reds with Structure	Ribera del Duero
Rich, Mineral-Driven Reds	Priorat (Catalonia)
Fortified & Complex Wines	Jerez (Sherry Country)

Wine Style	Go Here
Lush, Wild Mediterranean Reds	Valencia & Alicante
Earthy, Floral Reds	Bierzo (Mencía)
Sweet, Sun-Dried Wines	Montilla-Moriles (PX)
Volcanic & Funky Wines	Canary Islands

39

Wine Regions of Mainland Portugal
Transmontano VR
Trás-os-Montes DOC
Minho VR
Vinho Verde DOC
Duriense VR
Douro DOC
Porto DOC
Beira Atlântico VR
Bairrada DOC
Oporto
Terras de Cister VR
Távora-Varosa DOC
Lisboa VR
Bucelas DOC
Carcavelos DOC
Colares DOC
Lourinhã DOC
Óbidos DOC
Alenquer DOC
Arruda DOC
Torres Vedras DOC
Encostas d'Aire DOC
Terras do Dão VR
Dão DOC
Lafões DOC
Terras da Beira VR
Beira Interior DOC
Tejo VR
Do Tejo DOC
Lisbon
Alentejano VR
Alentejo DOC
Península de Setúbal VR
Setúbal DOC
Palmela DOC
Algarve VR
Lagos DOC
Portimão DOC
Lagoa DOC
Tavira DOC
Copyright: The Society of Wine Educators 2019

Portugal

40

Northern Portugal

Douro Valley

Famous For: Port Wine & Bold Dry Reds (Touriga Nacional, Touriga Franca)
Think: Blackberries, granite, sun-baked schist, and aged elegance. The Douro is Portugal's crown jewel—a UNESCO World Heritage site where vineyards cling to stone terraces carved into cliffs.
Port was once a favorite of British nobility, shipped downriver in rabelo boats.
Today, dry reds from Touriga Nacional are intense, aromatic, and ready to rival any Barolo or Bordeaux.

Major producers:

Symington Family Estates: Owns brands such as Graham's, Dow's, and Warre's, and has a historic presence with properties like Quinta do Bomfim. **Bridge family:** Owns the Taylor Fladgate brand. Sandeman: A large and well-known port wine brand with a property at Quinta do Seixo.
Ferreira and Fonseca: Historic producers with long legacies in the region.

Smaller and boutique producers

Quevedo: A family with generations of grape-growing experience that started creating their own wines in the 1990s.
Quinta do Pôpa: A winery that has recently converted to organic production.

Minho (Vinho Verde)

Famous For: Vinho Verde (Alvarinho, Loureiro) Think: Lime zest, green apple, river mist, and sea spray.
"Green Wine" isn't about color—it's about youth and freshness. These wines are light, crisp, and sometimes slightly fizzy.

Perfect with shellfish, sunshine, and summer breezes.

Some Minho **wine producers** include Quinta da Raza, Soalheiro, Anselmo Mendes, Avelada, and Quinta da Lixa. These producers are known for making a variety of wines, particularly Vinho Verde, which is a characteristic product of the region and often features grapes like Alvarinho and Loureiro.

41

Central Portugal

Dão

Famous For: Elegant Reds (Touriga Nacional, Tinta Roriz),
Encruzado whites
Think: Roses, pine forests, soft tannins, and slow charm.
Often called the "Burgundy of Portugal" for its refined, age-worthy reds. Granite soils and cooler mountain air give these wines balance and perfume.
Encruzado is one of Portugal's best-kept white secrets— floral, citrusy, and age-worthy.

Large-scale and historic producers:

Sogrape Vinhos: The largest producer in the Dão region and the largest Portuguese wine producer overall.
Casa da Ínsua: A winery in the Dão region that has been producing wine since 1908 and

is the only one in the region allowed to use some French grape varieties in its DOC wines.

Quinta de Lemos: Known for its wines made from indigenous Dão grape varieties and for being located near the 1-Star Michelin restaurant Mesa de Lemos.

Bairrada

Famous For: Baga (red), Sparkling Wines
Think: Black cherry, spice, and smoky earth.
Baga is a native powerhouse—tannic, tight, and built to last, like Nebbiolo's Portuguese cousin.
A region of rebels and revivalists, Bairrada is also Portugal's sparkling wine hotspot.

Some notable Bairrada wine producers include Adega de Cantanhede, the iconic Luis Pato, and Niepoort. Other producers are Vadio, Filipa Pato & William Wouters, V Puro, Quinta das Bágeiras, and Caves São João. These producers represent a mix of traditional methods, modern innovation, and a focus on indigenous grapes like Baga.

Lisboa (formerly Estremadura)

Famous For: Everything! Great value whites & reds

Think: Versatile, coastal, friendly.

This long Atlantic-facing region is one of Portugal's largest and most diverse.

From crisp Arinto to structured Castelão, there's a bottle for every table—often at budget-friendly prices.

Key producers:

Casa Santos Lima: One of the largest wine estates in Portugal, producing a wide variety of wines.

Adega Mãe: Located in Torres Vedras, it is part of the Riberalves Group.

Quinta de Chocapalha: A family-owned estate that replanted its vineyards and is known for its quality wines.

Manz Wines: An organic producer located near Mafra. **Adega Belém Urban Winery:** An urban winery in the Belém neighborhood of Lisbon, run by enologists David Picard and Catarina Moreira.

Quinta de Sant'Ana: An organic producer run by James and Ann Frost, located near Mafra.

Adega Regional de Colares: A producer from the historic Colares sub-region.
Quinta do Monte d'Oiro: Known for its wines from the coastal limestone hills.

Tejo

Famous For: Easy-drinking reds & whites
Think: Juicy, smooth, sun soaked.
Named after the **Tagus River**, Tejo wines are approachable and affordable.
This is everyday wine country: local, warm, and generous.

Notable producers in the Tejo region:

Quinta da Lapa: One of the oldest estates in the region, established in 1733.
Casal Branco: A traditional estate that dates to 1775.
Ode Winery: A modern, premium quality producer known for fruit-forward wines.
Adega de Almeirim: A cooperative that is one of the biggest producers of white wines in Portugal, particularly Fernão Pires.
Pedro Sereno: A new producer focusing on terroir-driven wines from the Tomar subregion.

Casal de Coelheira: A winery that blends traditional and modern methods, with a focus on indigenous grape varieties.

42

Southern Portugal

Alentejo

Famous For: Rich Reds (Alicante Bouschet, Aragonez), easy whites
Think: Black fruit, heat, leather, and wild herbs.
Vast and sun-drenched, Alentejo is Portugal's New World heart. **Alicante Bouschet** (a rare, red-fleshed grape) makes deeply colored, bold wines that are ready to impress.
Also known for traditional **amphora**-aged wine (vinho de talha).

Some Alentejo wine producers include Herdade dos Grous, João Portugal Ramos Wines, and Fitapreta Vinhos, along with larger estates like Herdade do Esporão and Sogrape. The region features a range of producers, from extensive, modern facilities to smaller family-owned operations.

Setúbal Peninsula

Famous For: Moscatel de Setúbal (fortified), Castelão **Think:** Orange blossom, caramelized figs, and coastal salinity. Moscatel de Setúbal is a sweet, fortified wine with rich, floral aromas—Portugal's answer to Muscat. **Castelão** thrives here too, making rustic, food-friendly reds.

Notable producers:

José Maria da Fonseca: A historic winery with a manor house and museum that has been in operation for nearly two centuries.
Casa Ermelinda Freitas: A winery established in 1920, located in Fernando Pó.
Quinta do Piloto: A family-run winery with over 200 hectares of vines, with history tracing back to 1900.
Quinta de Alcube: A winery situated in the heart of nature, known for its serene setting.

43

Portugal's Island Regions

Madeira

Famous For: Madeira Wine (fortified)
Think: Burnt sugar, roasted nuts, citrus peel, and an immortal shelf life. **Madeira wines** are intentionally oxidized and heated—they last forever and taste like sunshine. From dry Sercial to sweet Malmsey, these are wines for sipping, not gulping.

Prominent producers:

Henriques & Henriques: One of Madeira's most prestigious producers with over 160 years of tradition.
Blandy's: A family-owned company with over 210 years of experience.
H.M. Borges: A long-standing producer with a reputation for quality.
Pereira D'Oliveira: A respected name in the Madeira wine industry.
Cossart Gordon: The oldest established Madeira wine company, founded in 1745.

Azores (Açores)

Famous For: Minerally Whites (Arinto dos Açores, Verdelho)
Think: Sea salt, lemon rind, volcanic ash. Vines here grow in lava rock corrals to protect them from ocean winds. Wines are crisp, saline, and **rare,** produced in tiny quantities with a big personality.

Key producers in the Azores:

Azores Wine Company: Founded in 2014, this company was established to revive the potential of Azorean winemaking and indigenous grapes. It is known for its acclaimed Arinto dos Açores wine.
Pico Island Wine Cooperative (Picowines): Established in 1949, this is the oldest and largest wine producer in the Azores. It works with a network of local growers and is dedicated to preserving the traditional vineyard culture recognized by UNESCO.
Adega Cooperativa Dos Biscoitos, Crl: A cooperative producer is a significant winery in the region.

44

If You Like…

You Love This Style	Go Here
Bold, structured reds	Douro, Alentejo
Light, refreshing whites	Vinho Verde, Azores
Elegant, floral reds	Dão
Sparkling or funky	Bairrada, Lisboa
Fortified & historical	Madeira, Setúbal

45

Portugal Food & Wine Pairings by Region

Minho (Vinho Verde DOC)

Wine: Vinho Verde – Alvarinho, Loureiro
Pairing: Grilled sardines or bacalhau à brás.
Why it works: The tangy acidity, along with a light splash of Vinho Verde, cuts through the salty fish like a fresh breeze on a hot day.

Douro Valley

Wine: Dry red blends (Touriga Nacional, Touriga Franca), Port
Pairing: Posta à Mirandesa (grilled beef steak) or Queijo da Serra (sheep's cheese).
Why it works: Bold reds pair well with grilled meat, while aged Port complements salty-sweet cheese.

Dão

Wine: Elegant reds (Touriga Nacional), Encruzado whites
Pairing: Cabrito assado (roast goat).
Why it works: Dão's balance and finesse meet the richness of roast meat with subtle herbal lift.

Bairrada

Wine: Baga (red), traditional sparkling wine
Pairing: Leitão à Bairrada (roast suckling pig)
Why it works: High-acid Baga (or crisp sparkling) cuts through rich, fatty pork with mouthwatering precision.

Lisboa

Wine: Versatile blends, Arinto whites
Pairing: Amêijoas à Bulhão Pato (garlic-lemon clams)
Why it works: Zippy white wines amplify the flavors of lemon and herbs while cooling the heat of garlic.

Tejo

Wine: Fruity reds (Castelão), Fernão Pires whites
Pairing: Sopa da Pedra (hearty bean and sausage soup)
Why it works: Smooth reds and fuller-bodied whites pair well with rustic flavors and smoky sausage.

Setúbal Peninsula

Wine: Moscatel de Setúbal (fortified), Castelão
Pairing: Azeitão cheese or almond tarts
Why it works: Moscatel's floral sweetness plays beautifully with salty cheese and nutty sweets.

Alentejo

Wine: Full-bodied reds (Alicante Bouschet), Antão Vaz whites
Pairing: Carne de porco à Alentejana (pork with clams)
Why it works: Earthy reds ground the dish, while spicy, creamy whites echo the garlic and paprika.

Madeira (Island)

Wine: Madeira – Sercial (dry), Bual/Malmsey (sweet)
Pairing:
Sercial → grilled limpets (lapas)
Malmsey → bolo de mel (molasses cake)
Why it works: The fortified style pairs with either seafood salt or dessert spice—pick your bottle!

Azores (Açores)

Wine: Arinto dos Açores
Pairing: Cracas (barnacles) or tuna steak with sweet potato Why it works: Mineral-driven whites pair perfectly with volcanic seafood and earthy root veggies.

46

Cheat Sheet: What to Eat...

Dish	Drink This
Grilled fish or sardines	Vinho Verde (Minho)
Roast meat or lamb	Touriga Nacional
Shellfish & garlic dishes	(Douro or Dão)
Pork with clams	Arinto (Lisboa or Tejo)
Portuguese cheese	Alicante Bouschet or Antão Vaz (Alentejo)
Salted cod (bacalhau)	Encruzado or dry Madeira
Desserts (almonds, honey)	Moscatel or Malmsey (Madeira)

47

Germany and Austria

Wine Regions of Germany

Wine Regions of Austria

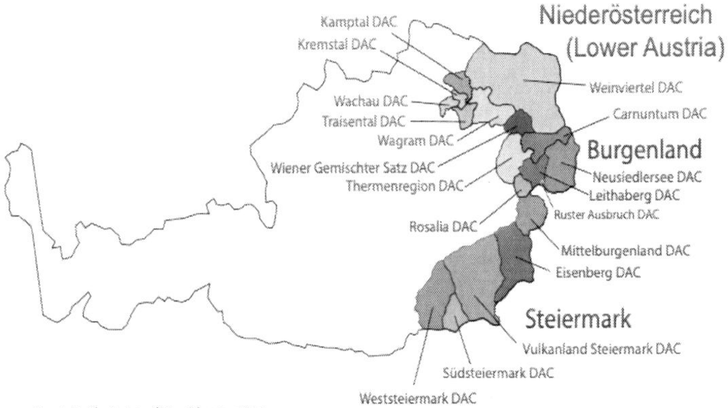

48

Germany

Mosel

Famous For: Riesling (Dry to Lusciously Sweet)
Think: Green apple, slate, citrus zest, and crystalline purity.
These wines are like poetry written in acidity. Mosel's steep vineyard slopes are some of the most dramatic in the world—harvested by hand, sometimes with ropes.
Fun Fact: Some Rieslings from the Mosel can age gracefully for 50 years or more.
Bonus: even sweet versions have enough acid to cut through pork belly or Thai curry.

Some of the top Mosel wine producers include Joh. Jos. Prüm, Weingut Dr. Loosen, Weingut Willi Schaefer, and Markus Molitor. Other highly-regarded estates, many of which are members of the VDP (Verband Deutscher Prädikatsweingüter), include Selbach-Oster,

Clemens Busch, Carl Loewen, and Van Volxem.

Rheingau

Famous For: Dry Riesling, Spätburgunder (Pinot Noir)
Think: Peach skin, herbs, and a serious backbone.
Rheingau's Rieslings are dry and structured, making them ideal for pairing with food and aging.
And yes—Germany makes red wine! **Spätburgunder** here is Pinot with a crisp, foresty twist.

Renowned Rheingau producers:

Weingut Georg Breuer: A very popular and highly-regarded estate in Rüdesheim.
Weingut Robert Weil: A prestigious producer, known for its excellent Rieslings.
Schloss Vollrads: One of the world's oldest wine estates, with a long history of producing fine wines.
Kloster Eberbach (Staatsweingüter Eltville): This historic estate produces some

of the region's most famous and high- quality Rieslings.

Weingut August Kesseler: Another top-tier producer in the Rheingau region.

Weingut Balthasar Ress: A popular and highly-rated organic estate located in Hattenheim.

J.B. Becker: Considered a favorite among experts for his Rheingau wines.

Weingut August Eser: A well-known producer in the Rheingau, with a strong reputation.

Pfalz

Famous For: Full-Bodied Riesling, Pinot Gris, Dornfelder

Think: Sun-soaked vineyards, generous fruit, and approachability. Pfalz is the warmest central wine region in Germany—Rieslings here are rounder, riper, and sometimes more floral.

Also home to serious **Pinot** family wines (Blanc, Gris, and Noir), as well as red-wine experimentation.

Top Pfalz wine producers:

Weingut Dr. Bürklin-Wolf: An historic estate dating back to 1597, it is a pioneer in high-quality Riesling and is committed to organic and biodynamic farming.
Weingut Reichsrat von Buhl: Known for producing top-quality Riesling since 1849 and owning one of the most impressive vineyard collections in the region.
Weingut Friedrich Becker: A successful estate that has focused on winegrowing since 1973, particularly noted for its red wines, like Spätburgunder (Pinot Noir).
Weingut Langenwalter: This winery is known for aging its wines in local Pfalz oak barrels and producing a wide range of wines, including exceptional reds and Riesling.

Franken (Franconia)

Famous For: Silvaner

Think: Herbal, earthy, and slightly salty.

Silvaner in a bocksbeutel (that flat, round bottle) is Franken's calling card.

Great with asparagus, mushrooms, and other green, earthy foods.

The top Franken (Franconia) wine producers are known for their high-quality, characterful dry white wines, especially those made from the Silvaner grape. Key producers include prestigious historic estates and modern, quality-focused wineries. Many of the best wines come in the distinctive, flask- shaped Bocksbeutel bottle.

Baden

Famous For: Spätburgunder (Pinot Noir), Grauburgunder (Pinot Gris)
Think: Ripe fruit, smoky depth, and warm-climate finesse. Baden sits just across the Rhine from Alsace and shares a love of aromatic whites and **Pinot Noir**, but with a bit of extra sun and richness.

Weingut Bernhard Huber:

Known for Spätburgunder, with wines like the Malterdingen Wildenstein Spätburgunder GG earning high accolades.

Weingut Dr. Heger:

A prominent winery producing top-tier Spätburgunder and Weißburgunder, including the highly-rated "Gras im Ofen" GG from the Ihringer Winklerberg vineyard.

Weingut Salwey:

Produces both red and white wines from its Oberrotweil vineyards, with well-regarded examples including the Steingrubenberg Weißburgunder GG and Henkenberg Grauburgunder GG.

Weingut Hanspeter Ziereisen:

Specializes in white wines like Gutedel, with the "Jaspis 10hoch4" being a noted example.

49

Austria

Wachau

Famous For: Grüner Veltliner, Riesling
Think: White pepper, lemon peel, stone, and spine. Wachau wines are laser-focused and mineral-driven, built to age and shine at the table.
Grüner Veltliner here = Austria's signature grape.
Fun Fact: The region uses a special quality scale: Steinfeder (light), Federspiel (medium), Smaragd (rich & age-worthy).

About Wachau wine:

Grapes: The region is famous for full-bodied, complex white wines, particularly Grüner Veltliner and Riesling.
Vinea Wachau Nobilis Districtus: A quality association that classifies wines into three dry styles:

Steinfeder: Lightest style with a maximum of 11.5% alcohol. **Federspiel:** Medium-bodied wines between 11.5% and 12.5% alcohol. **Smaragd:** The most powerful and age-worthy wines, with a minimum of 12.5% alcohol.

Kamptal & Kremstal

Famous For: Grüner Veltliner, Riesling
Think: Green apple, radish, and high-tone citrus. Cooler than Wachau, but no less elegant. Kamptal's wines often exhibit more herbaceousness, while Kremstal wines offer a touch more roundness.
Both regions are adjacent to the famous **Wachau** and share similar Danube River influence, but each has a distinct character.

Top Kamptal producers:

Weingut Bründlmayer:
Recognized as a "star wine producer" and "beacon of Austrian viticulture," Bründlmayer is a family-owned winery with roots dating back to 1792. Led by Willi Bründlmayer, the vineyards are farmed organically and located on hillsides and terraces around Langenlois.
Schloss Gobelsburg:

One of the oldest wineries in Europe, with a heritage dating back to the 12th century. The estate was managed by monks until 1996 and is now run by Michael and Eva Moosbrugger. They follow sustainable practices, including organic farming.

Weingut Hirsch:

A family-owned winery since the 16th century, run by Josef and Johannes Hirsch. They are known for their minimal intervention winemaking, ambient yeast fermentation, and slow vinification. The winery focuses exclusively on Grüner Veltliner and Riesling.

Burgenland

Famous For: Blaufränkisch (red), Zweigelt, Sweet Wines

Think: Dark cherry, spice, and lakeside generosity. Burgenland, bordering Hungary, brings the red wine heat to Austria. Blaufränkisch = Austria's answer to Syrah, with peppery finesse. Also, home to **Ruster Ausbruch**, a legendary botrytized dessert wine.

Noteable Producers:

Weingut Hans Igler: A family-run winery with over 50 years of experience, known for high-quality wines with a philosophy that starts in the vineyards. They are a notable producer of Blaufränkisch in the Mittelburgenland region, where the climate is hot in summer and cold in winter, and heavy clay soils store water for the vines.
Salzl Seewinkelhof: Located in the Seewinkel area, this winery is surrounded by the Seewinkel National Park and is famous for its warm and soft wines. The winery also offers a four-star guest house and a pool, making it a popular destination for wine tourism.
Christian Tschida: A producer particularly noted for his innovative approach to making wines from both local and international grapes, with a focus on red wines like Cabernet Franc. His wines are highly sought after for their quality and unique expression, as seen in bottlings like "Non-Tradition Red".
Heinrich: Considered one of Austria's most innovative producers, Heinrich makes lively wines with a focus on freshness and lower alcohol.

Styria (Steiermark

Famous For: Sauvignon Blanc, Gelber Muskateller, Schilcher

Think: Mountain herbs, alpine flowers, and citrus lift. Wines here are zippy, aromatic, and joyfully fresh.

Schilcher (from the Blauer Wildbacher grape) is a tangy rosé found nowhere else.

Producers:

Weingut Tement: An internationally acclaimed estate in South Styria, known for its outstanding single-vineyard wines, particularly the Zieregg Sauvignon Blanc.

Weingut Neumeister: A top-tier winery whose wines are imported by Rosenthal Wine Merchants. It is a family business located in the Vulkanland Steiermark sub-region.

Weingut Erwin Sabathi: From South Styria, this winery has a winemaking tradition since 1650. The family produces a range of excellent Sauvignon Blanc and Chardonnay wines, with grapes grown on the Pössnitzberg vineyard.

Weingut Sattlerhof: Along with Tement, this winery is considered one of Austria's best producers.

Weingut Lackner-Tinnacher: This winery is noted for its classic, terroir-driven wines.

Weingut Muster (Sepp & Maria Muster): A renowned producer of biodynamic and natural wines in South Styria. They are part of the "Schmecke Das Leben" group of biodynamic growers.

Thermenregion

Famous For: Zierfandler, Rotgipfler (native whites)
Think: Almond, citrus rind, subtle spice.
This historic region, located just **south of Vienna**, produces rare indigenous whites with creamy textures and exceptional aging potential.

Top **wine producers** include Weingut Familie Reinisch, Weingut Hartl, and Weingut Stadlmann. Other prominent wineries are Weingut Alphart, Weingut Christian Fischer, and Weingut Biegler. These producers are known for their quality, with Reinisch focusing on Burgundy varieties like Pinot Noir and Hartl being a leader in both reds and the local Rotgipfler and Zierfandler white grapes.

50

Germany & Austria– Food & Wine Pairings by Region

Mosel

Wine: Riesling (dry to sweet)
Pairing: Roast pork with apple, or spicy Thai curry.
Why it works: The crisp acidity and gentle sweetness balance heat, fat, and fruit, making it crazy versatile.

Rheingau

Wine: Dry Riesling, Spätburgunder (Pinot Noir)
Pairing:
Riesling: Smoked trout or Wiener schnitzel
Spätburgunder: Roast duck or mushroom risotto.
Why it works: The structure in the wines is perfect for smoky, savory, or umami-rich dishes.

Pfalz

Wine: Full-bodied Riesling, Pinot Gris, Dornfelder
Pairing: Sausage platter (Bratwurst, Leberwurst) with mustard and kraut.
Why it works: The generous fruit and fuller body of Pfalz wines balance out the richness and saltiness.

Franken (Franconia)

Wine: Silvaner
Pairing: White asparagus with hollandaise or herbed pork loin.
Why it works: Silvaner's earthy-mineral profile enhances spring vegetables and gentle herbs.

Baden

Wine: Spätburgunder, Grauburgunder (Pinot Gris)
Pairing: Black Forest ham or grilled veal chop.
Why it works: Baden's richer climate yields bolder wines that pair with charcuterie and grilled meats.

Austria – Food & Wine Pairings by Region

Wachau

Wine: Grüner Veltliner, Riesling
Pairing: Wiener Schnitzel or roast chicken with lemon and herbs.
Why it works: Grüner's peppery zip and citrus cut through fried or fatty foods beautifully.

Kamptal & Kremstal

Wine: Grüner Veltliner, Riesling
Pairing: Fresh goat cheese, spring greens, or herbed fish.
Why it works: These cool-climate wines are bright, green, and clean—perfect with fresh, light fare.

Burgenland

Wine: Blaufränkisch, Zweigelt, Ruster Ausbruch (sweet)
Pairing:
Blaufränkisch: Grilled lamb or duck with cherry glaze. Zweigelt: Stuffed cabbage or paprika chicken. Ruster Ausbruch: Blue cheese or apricot tart.

Why it works: Red wines pair well with spice and game; sweet wines complement and contrast with salty or tangy desserts.

Styria (Steiermark)

Wine: Sauvignon Blanc, Gelber Muskateller, Schilcher
Pairing: Pumpkin seed oil salad, trout, or alpine cheeses.
Why it works: High-acid, aromatic wines pair perfectly with mountain cuisine and fresh herbs.

Thermenregion

Wine: Zierfandler, Rotgipfler (indigenous whites)
Pairing: Veal ragout or creamy spaetzle with herbs.
Why it works: These textural, layered whites handle creamy dishes with ease—rare grapes, refined results.

51

Bonus Cheat Sheet

Wine Region	Best Pairing
Mosel	Pork + apples or spicy food
Rheingau	Smoked trout, roast duck
Franken	White asparagus, pork with herbs
Baden	Veal, Black Forest ham
Wachau	Wiener Schnitzel, roast chicken
Kamptal/Kremstal	Goat cheese, herbed fish
Burgenland	Grilled meats, paprika dishes, and blue cheese

Wine Region	Best Pairing
Styria	Trout, pumpkin oil salad, alpine cheeses
Thermenregion	Veal ragout, creamy spaetzle

52

South America - Argentina

Famous For: Malbec (especially from Mendoza)

Think: Plums, violets, mountain air, and steak dinners.
Mendoza sits at the foothills of the Andes, where high altitude and intense sunlight combine to produce deeply colored, lush reds with smooth tannins. Malbec was once a French blending grape, but in Argentina found its soulmate terroir. Some vineyards sit above 1,500 meters (5,000 ft)

Main Wine Areas of Argentina

Mendoza

Grapes: Malbec, Cabernet Sauvignon, Bonarda, Torrontés
Vibe: High-altitude sun, stony soils, and bold reds
Fun Fact: Some of the world's highest vineyards are in Uco Valley—over 1,500m (5,000 ft)!
Styles: Powerful yet polished Malbecs, floral Torrontés, mineral-driven whites.

Notable Vineyards:

Catena Zapata:
Founded in 1902 by Italian immigrant Nicola Catena, Catena Zapata is arguably Argentina's most famous and influential winery. The winery is known for its six historic vineyards, primarily the Adrianna Vineyard in the Gualtallary sub-region of the Uco Valley. At over 1,450 meters (4,750 feet) in altitude, it is referred to as Argentina's "Grand Cru" and has received numerous perfect scores from critics.
Bodega Zuccardi Valle de Uco:
A family-owned winery with roots in Maipú since 1963, Zuccardi is widely recognized for its high-altitude wines from the Uco Valley. Terroir focus: Winemaking is led by Sebastián Zuccardi, who has a passionate focus on

expressing the unique character of the Uco Valley's diverse soils and microclimates.

Viña Cobos:

Established in 1999 by American winemaker Paul Hobbs and his partners, Viña Cobos has quickly become a benchmark for luxury Malbec in Argentina. Having consulted for Catena in the late 1980s, Hobbs was an early believer in Mendoza's potential for high-end wines and established Viña Cobos to explore single-vineyard expressions.

Salta

Grapes: Torrontés, Malbec Altitude: Up to 3,000m (9,800 ft) – the highest commercial vineyards in the world!

Vibe: Intense sun, cool nights = wines with perfume and edge.

Fun Fact: Torrontés from Cafayate is Argentina's most aromatic white. Many of the top producers are in the Calchaquí Valley, which is home to some of the highest commercial vineyards in the world.

Vineyards to see:

Bodega Colomé:

The oldest operating winery in Argentina, founded in 1831 by the Spanish governor of Salta. It was later acquired by Swiss entrepreneur Donald Hess in 2001, who significantly invested in the winery and community. Colomé is home to the world's highest commercial vineyard, Altura Máxima, planted at a staggering 3,111 meters (over 10,200 feet) above sea level. Grapes grown at such high altitudes develop thick skins, resulting in wines with concentrated flavor, color, and supple tannins.

Bodega El Esteco: Established: Founded in 1892 by French immigrants, this winery is located in the heart of the Calchaquí Valley. Its high-altitude vineyards benefit from low rainfall, natural irrigation, and significant temperature variations between day and night, producing beautifully balanced wines.

Bodega San Pedro de Yacochuya: Developed in collaboration between Salta winemaker Arnaldo Etchart and renowned French consultant Michel Rolland. Specializing in powerful, barrel-aged red varietals, primarily from 60-year-old vines. Their premium Yacochuya Malbec (often blended with a hint of Cabernet Sauvignon) is one of the most respected wines in the region.

Yacochuya wines were the first in Argentina to be barrel-fermented.

Patagonia

Grapes: Pinot Noir, Merlot, Malbec
Vibe: Windswept plains, low humidity, and elegant reds Fun Fact: One of the best places in South America for fresh, balanced Pinot.

Top Patagonia wine producers include Bodega Chacra, known for world-class Pinot Noir and Chardonnay, and Familia Schroeder, a major producer famous for its Malbecs and Cabernet Sauvignon. Other notable producers are Humberto Canale, a historic winery founded in 1909, and Bodega NQN, which is now part of Bodega Malma and has gained recognition for its quality wines.

53

South America – Chile

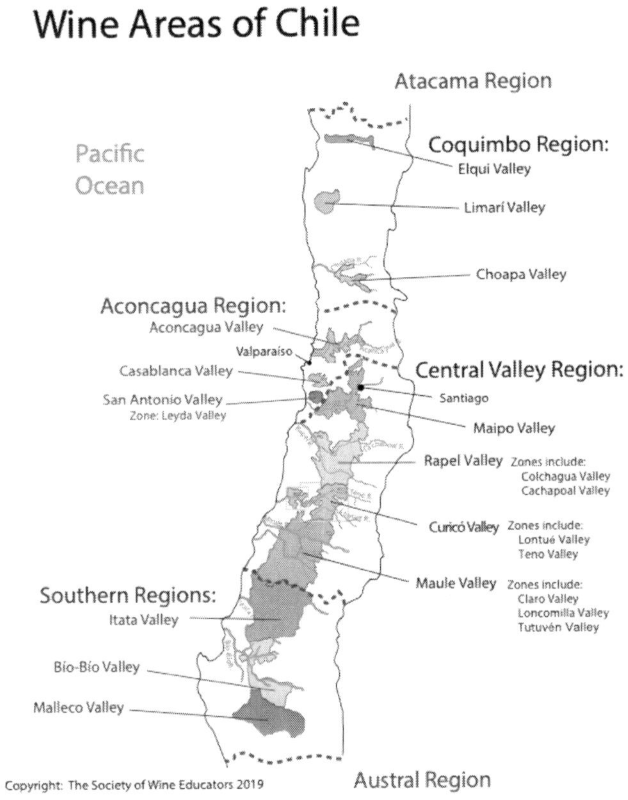

Maipo Valley

Grapes: Cabernet Sauvignon, Carménère
Vibe: Warm, structured reds with herbal complexity
Fun Fact: Home to Chile's oldest vines and biggest producers.

Concha y Toro:
The largest wine producer in Latin America, globally recognized for its "Don Melchor" Cabernet Sauvignon. Founded in 1883, it has become a classic and popular destination for wine tours.
Santa Rita:
Founded in 1880, it is considered one of Chile's quintessential wine estates, known for its elegant "Casa Real" wines. It has historic importance, with its vineyards developed during the period of French-influenced winemaking.
Cousiño Macul:
A historic and family-run winery, established in 1856, that continues to produce high-quality red wines.

Undurraga:
One of the oldest and largest wineries in Chile, with an extensive portfolio. Notable for its Terroir Hunter series, sparkling wines, and historic garden featuring centenary trees at its Maipo winery.

Colchagua Valley

Grapes: Carménère, Syrah, Cabernet
Vibe: Lush, smooth reds with dark fruit and chocolate notes.
Fun Fact: Carménère thrives here, often **mistaken** for Merlot until the 1990s.

Premier producers:

Casa Lapostolle: Famous for its Clos Apalta wine, which is considered one of the most prestigious wines from the valley.
Montes: An iconic producer known for its Folly Syrah. The winery is known for its unique Feng Shui architecture and offers a restaurant overlooking the vineyards.
Viña Casa Silva: A well-regarded producer that makes the "Altura" wine, showcasing the high quality of the region.

Casablanca Valley

Grapes: Sauvignon Blanc, Chardonnay, Pinot Noir
Vibe: Ocean-cooled vineyards = crisp, aromatic whites and elegant reds.
Fun Fact: Often compared to **Sonoma** for its coastal climate.

Top wine producers in Casablanca Valley:
Casas del Bosque: A leading winery in the region, founded in 1993, known for its Sauvignon Blanc and Pinot Noir. It features the popular Tanino restaurant and offers activities like bike rides and picnics.
Matetic Winery: Famous for its organic and biodynamic wines and offers a modern, elegant setting for personalized tours and tastings.
Villard Fine Wines: A boutique estate founded in 1989 by Thierry Villard, now run by his son, Jean-Charles. It's known for its high-quality and elegant wines, and the family personally leads tours.
Emiliana Organic Vineyards: A highly-rated winery known for its organic wines.
Veramonte Winery: Known for its organic wines and meticulous soil care. The estate also offers activities like bike tours and picnics.

Cono Sur: Well-known for its Pinot Noir, which is often compared to Burgundy wines.
Casa Lapostolle: Considered one of the most famous wine producers in the valley.
Concha Y Toro: One of the first companies to produce high-quality white wines in the region.

Leyda & San Antonio

Grapes: Sauvignon Blanc, Pinot Noir
Vibe: Precision, minerality, and salty sea spray
Fun Fact: Wines from here often have a saline, oyster-shell edge, grand with seafood
The Leyda Valley is a sub-region of San Antonio, with its closer proximity to the Pacific Ocean resulting in a distinct, cool, and mineral-driven coastal style.

Top producers in the Leyda and San Antonio Valleys:

Viña Leyda: The pioneering winery of the Leyda Valley, founded in 1998, is particularly acclaimed as a master of Pinot Noir. Other notable varietals include Sauvignon Blanc, Chardonnay, and Syrah.
Viña Garcés Silva (Amayna/Boya):

An early investor in the Leyda sub-region, the Garcés Silva family produces wines under the labels Amayna and Boya. Amayna wines are described as opulent and barrel-aged, while the Boya label offers fresh, fruit-forward wines.

Viña Casa Marin:

Known for its expressive and exclusive wines that highlight the unique terroir of Lo Abarca, a sub-region of San Antonio. Winemaker María Luz Marín focuses on varietals such as Riesling, Sauvignon Gris, and Gewürztraminer.

Matetic Vineyards:

This winery, located in the San Antonio Valley, is a top producer of biodynamic wines. It is especially known for its Syrah and Sauvignon Blanc.

54

South America Cheat Sheet

Chile

Wine Style	Go Here
Cool-Climate Reds	Casablanca Valley (Pinot Noir)
Crisp Coastal Whites	San Antonio & Leyda Valleys (Sauvignon Blanc)
Rich, Fruit-Forward Reds	Colchagua Valley (Carmenère, Syrah)
Elegant Cabernet Sauvignon	Maipo Valley

Wine Style	Go Here
High-Altitude Reds	Cachapoal & Aconcagua
Old Vine Heritage Wines	Maule Valley (Carignan)
Natural & Experimental	Itata Valley

Argentina

Wine Style	Go Here
Iconic Malbec	Mendoza (Uco Valley)
High-Elevation Elegance	Salta (Malbec, Torrontés)

Wine Style	Go Here
Bright, Floral Whites	Cafayate (Torrontés)
Age-Worthy, Structured Reds	Luján de Cuyo
Patagonian Cool-Climate Reds	(Malbec, Cabernet)
Sparkling & Aromatic Styles	Río Negro & Neuquén (Pinot Noir)
Old Vine Bonarda & Criolla	San Rafael (Chardonnay, Cheni San Juan & La Rioja (Argentina

55

South America Food & Wine Pairings

Argentina

Mendoza (Malbec, Cabernet Sauvignon)
Pairing: Bife de chorizo (ribeye steak) with chimichurri.
Why it works: Malbec's juicy richness pairs well with grilled beef; the acidity complements the herbs in the sauce.

Salta (Torrontés, Malbec)
Pairing: Empanadas salteñas (spiced meat turnovers).
Why it works: Torrontés balances the savory filling with floral lift and crisp acidity.

Patagonia (Pinot Noir, Merlot)
Pairing: Cordero patagónico (Patagonian lamb).

Why it works: Earthy, elegant Pinot complements the smoky, herb-roasted meat.

Chile

Maipo Valley (Cabernet Sauvignon
Pairing: Lomo a lo pobre (steak with fries, onions, and egg).
Why it works: The cab's structure pairs well with the richness of the dish and cuts through the fried edges.

Colchagua Valley (Carménère, Syrah
Pairing: Pastel de choclo (corn pie with beef and olives).
Why it works: Carménère's sweet pepper notes echo the corn while tannins match the meat.

Casablanca Valley (Sauvignon Blanc, Chardonnay)
Pairing: Ceviche de reineta (white fish marinated in citrus).
Why it works: Sauvignon Blanc's citrus and salt tones amplify the freshness of the fish.

Leyda/San Antonio (Pinot Noir, Sauvignon Blanc)

Pairing: Locos con mayo (Chilean abalone with mayo).
Why it works: Mineral whites and delicate reds complement the briny, creamy contrast.

56

South American Pairing Cheat Sheet

Country	Region	Wine	Dish
Argentina	Mendoza	Malbec	Grilled steak with chimichurri
Argentina	Salta	Torrontés	Spiced beef empanadas
Chile	Colchagua	Carménère	Corn pie with meat (pastel de choclo)
Chile	Casablanca	Sauvignon Blanc	Ceviche

57

Australia

Selected Wine Areas of Australia

58

South Australia

Barossa Valley

Famous For: Shiraz
Think: Blackberry jam, black pepper, eucalyptus, and old-vine intensity.
Barossa is Australia's iconic red wine region, home to some of the oldest productive vines in the world— some dating back to the **1840s**. Shiraz here is bold, rich, and full-bodied, with warm sun and deep spice in every sip.

Top Barossa Valley wine producers, including Henschke, Yalumba, Langmeil Winery, Seppeltsfield, Rockford, and Chateau Tanunda, are renowned for their historic significance and high-quality wines, particularly Shiraz made from old vines. Other notable wineries include Grant Burge, Elderton Wines, and those within the Artisans of Barossa collective, which specializes in small-batch winemaking.

Eden Valley

Famous For: Riesling
Think: Lime zest, wet stone, and electric acidity.
Eden sits at a higher elevation, giving a zippy, bone-dry Riesling style that can age for decades.
Fun Fact: Riesling from Eden **can age 20+ years** and develop flavors of toast, honey, and lanolin—while still bone dry!

Top Eden Valley wine producers include Henschke, Yalumba, and Rockford, known for high-quality Shiraz and Riesling. Other notable producers include Pewsey Vale Vineyard, Heggies Vineyard, and boutique wineries such as Flaxman Wines and Fernfield Wines, which offer a more personal, smaller scale tasting experience. These wineries highlight the region's reputation for cooler-climate-style wines due to its higher elevation and cooler temperatures compared to the nearby Barossa Valley.

Clare Valley

Famous For: Riesling

Think: Lemon-lime, talc, and white florals. These wines are refreshing, crisp, and mineral-driven— perfect for pairing with spicy food or warm days.
Australia's signature dry Riesling style starts here.
Fun Fact: The famous Riesling Trail is a **35-km walking/ biking path** connecting cellar doors along an old railway line.

Jim Barry:
A pioneer in the region, highly respected for both its premium Riesling and high-concentration Shiraz.
Grosset:
A highly acclaimed producer primarily known for its outstanding Riesling but also produces a subtle and refined Shiraz using organic and certified Biodynamic farming practices.
Kilikanoon:
Specialty: Known for its award-winning Shiraz, which displays classic dark fruit and spice characteristics.
Taylors (Wakefield):
One of the region's most important winemakers, producing fruit-driven, supple-textured wines in the masstige/premium

market, and known for fruit-driven wines with supple textures.

McLaren Vale

Famous For: Grenache, Shiraz, Cabernet
Think: Red berries, baking spices, and a fresh sea breeze—one of the oldest wine regions in the country, but a hotbed of experimentation, too. Grenache is the rising star here. Fun Fact: One of the few regions in the world with over **40 different soil types**—in one valley!

Top McLaren Vale **wine producers** include d'Arenberg, known for the iconic d'Arenberg Cube; Wirra Wirra Vineyards, a historic winery celebrated for its Shiraz; and Coriole Vineyards, noted for its Italian varietals and picturesque setting. Other notable producers include Gemtree Wines, known for its biodynamic approach, Mollydooker Wines, and Oliver's Taranga Vineyards, a family-owned estate offering an innovative wine selection.

Adelaide Hills

Famous For: Chardonnay, Sauvignon Blanc, Pinot Noir
Think: Bright acidity, white peach, and cool-climate elegance. Close to the city but elevated and breezy. Think Aussie Burgundy vibes with a chill attitude.
Fun Fact: This is Australia's sparkling wine frontier, with altitude-driven freshness and a **strong focus on sustainability.**

Established and well-known producers:

Shaw and Smith: A major player in the region, considered one of Australia's most respected producers.
Nepenthe: A benchmark winery for premium, quality wines that are recognized globally.
Longview Vineyard: A family-owned winery that has earned high ratings.
Boutique and award-winning producers:
Gentle Folk: Known for its Piccadilly Chardonnay 2023, which has been highlighted as one of the best wines from the region.

CRFT: Recognized for its K1 Vineyard Kuitpo Grüner Veltliner 2024 and is also listed as a sustainable producer.
Mt Lofty Ranges Vineyard: An award-winning, family-owned winery with spectacular views, specializing in cool-climate Chardonnay and Pinot Noir.

59

Victoria

Yarra Valley

Famous For: Pinot Noir, Chardonnay
Think: Red cherries, mushrooms, citrus peel. Elegant, silky, and Burgundy-inspired, but proudly Aussie. It is also home to some of the country's best sparkling wines. Fun Fact: **Victoria was the first wine region in Australia,** dating back to 1838, and was later revived in the 1960s after being forgotten for decades.

Top Yarra Valley wine producers include Coldstream Hills, De Bortoli Wines, and Yering Station, which are known for their quality cool-climate wines like Pinot Noir and Chardonnay.
Other highly-regarded estates are Yarra Yering, Seville Estate, and Levantine Hill Estate, the latter of which has produced one

of Australia's most expensive new-release wines.

Mornington Peninsula

Famous For: Pinot Noir
Think: Rose petals, strawberry, ocean spray.
With vineyards cooled by the sea, this is coastal Pinot perfection—light, delicate, food-loving.
Fun Fact: Surrounded by water on three sides, it gets **natural air conditioning**—ideal for delicate Pinot and Chardonnay.
Top Mornington Peninsula wine producers include Paringa Estate for its award-winning cool-climate Shiraz and Pinot Noir, Crittenden for being an iconic and long-standing family winery, and Ocean Eight for its elegant, cool-climate wines. Main Ridge Estate is the region's oldest operational winery, first releasing wine in 1980. Rahona Valley is a boutique producer specializing in premium sparkling wines.

Rutherglen

Famous For: Fortified Muscat
Think: Raisins, toffee, orange peel.

Some of the world's sweetest and richest dessert wines are made here, aged for decades in **solera systems.**
Fun Fact: Rutherglen's Muscat of Rutherglen is often called the "liquid gold" of dessert wines and can be **over 100 years old** in the blend!

All Saints Estate:
Founded in 1864, it is one of Australia's oldest wineries. It produces a wide range of high-quality fortified and still wines, including those from old-vine plantings like Shiraz (1920) and Muscat (1930).
Campbells Wines:
A historic winery with fifth-generation family ownership. Known for a diverse portfolio of reds, whites, rosés, and sparkling wines, with particular fame for its fortified wines like the Rutherglen Muscat.
Chambers Rosewood Vineyards:
Founded in 1858, it is one of Rutherglen's most revered wineries. The sixth generation of the Chambers family now runs it.
Pfeiffer Wines:
Known for its high-quality wines, including those from its historic distillery.

60

New South Wales

Hunter Valley

Famous For: Semillon
Think: Lemon curd, beeswax, lanolin.
Young: bright and citrusy.
Aged: toasty and complex.
Hunter Semillon is Australia's most incredible white wine sleeper hit.
Fun Fact: Australia's oldest continuous wine region—
James Busby planted the first vines in the **1820s**, many of which are still descendants of European cuttings.

Top Hunter Valley **wine producers** include historical giants like Tyrrell's Wines and Brokenwood Wines, renowned for their premium and signature Shiraz, and boutique producers like Thomas Wines and Briar Ridge Vineyard, known for their single-vineyard and high-quality wines. Other notable wineries are

Keith Tulloch Wine, McGuigan Wines, and Hungerford Hill, each offering unique experiences and acclaimed products.

Orange & Canberra District

Famous For: Cool-climate Shiraz, Chardonnay, Viognier
Think: Spice, structure, and altitude-driven freshness. These regions are on the rise, producing refined, food-friendly wines at **elevation**.

Top **wine producers** in the Orange & Canberra District include Clonakilla, Helm Wines, and Shaw Wines, known for their Shiraz and Riesling. Other highly-regarded wineries in the region are Four Winds Vineyard, Lark Hill Winery, and Mount Majura Vineyard, which are praised for a range of cool-climate wines and their cellar door experiences.

61

Western Australia

Margaret River

Famous For: Cabernet Sauvignon, Chardonnay, Sauvignon Blanc-Semillon blends
Think: Cassis, bay leaf, lemon butter, sea salt. With a **maritime climate like Bordeaux**, Margaret River is punching way above its size—serious wines with balance and poise.

Founding and iconic wineries:

Vasse Felix: Established in 1967, it is the oldest winery in the Margaret River region. Virginia Willcock is the award-winning winemaker.
Leeuwin Estate: Another of the founding wineries, its origins were guided by Robert Mondavi in 1972, who helped transform the property into a world-class winery. **Cullen Wines:** With Vanya Cullen as chief

winemaker, the family-owned estate is known for its high-quality wines, blending tradition with modern techniques.
Cape Mentelle: A founding winery that was established in 1970.

Great Southern

Famous For: Riesling, Shiraz, and Pinot Noir. **Think:** Wild herbs, firm acidity, forest berries. Cool-climate magic + large-scale isolation = **hidden gems** with elegance.

Top Great Southern wine producers include Plantagenet Wines, Howard Park, and West Cape Howe Wines, known for their historical significance and quality wines. Plantagenet is a pioneer focused on finesse. At the same time, Howard Park is a pioneer in traditional method sparkling wines, and West Cape Howe consistently produces award-winning, balanced wines from the region's oldest plantings. Other notable producers are Gilbert Wines, Ferngrove Wines, and Galafrey Wines.

62

Tasmania

Famous For: Sparkling wine, Pinot Noir, Chardonnay

Think: Strawberry, sea spray, oyster shells. Tasmania has become Australia's sparkling wine capital, with climate and soils perfect for Champagne-style fizz and graceful **Pinots**. It's the cool-climate frontier— and it's booming.

Top Tasmanian wine producers include Josef Chromy Wines, known for its sparkling wines and Pinot Noir, and Pooley Wines, recognized as a leading cool-climate producer. Other prominent producers are Jansz Tasmania, celebrated for its prestige sparkling wines, such as the Premium Cuvée, and Stoney Rise, which focuses on cool-climate varietals like Pinot Noir and Chardonnay. Many of these wineries are in regions such as the Tamar Valley, the Coal River Valley, and the East Coast.

63

Australia Cheat Sheet:

You Love This Style	Go Here
Bold, spicy reds	Barossa, McLaren Vale
Cool-climate Pinot & Chard	Yarra Valley, Tasmania
Dry, zesty whites	Clare Valley, Eden Valley
Rich dessert wines	Rutherglen
Structured, elegant reds	Margaret River, Canberra
Sparkling finesse	Tasmania, Yarra Valley

64

Wine & Food Pairings

South Australia

Barossa Valley
Wine: Shiraz
Pairing: Slow-roasted lamb with rosemary & garlic.
Why: Bold meat meets bold wine — peppery Shiraz complements rich, savory flavors.

Eden Valley
Wine: Dry Riesling
Pairing: Fresh oysters with lime.
Why: The zippy acidity cuts through brine and brightens the shellfish like a squeeze of citrus.

Clare Valley
Wine: Riesling
Pairing: Spicy Thai green curry.
Why: Dry but fruity Riesling handles heat like a champ and balances sweet-spice flavor bombs.

McLaren Vale
Wine: Grenache
Pairing: Charcuterie board with aged cheddar and prosciutto.
Why: Juicy red fruit + spicy edges + savory snacks = wine night perfection.

Adelaide Hills
Wine: Sauvignon Blanc or Chardonnay
Pairing: Goat cheese salad with lemon vinaigrette.
Why: Bright wine + tangy cheese = clean, crisp, and refreshing harmony.

Victoria

Yarra Valley
Wine: Pinot Noir
Pairing: Duck breast with cherry glaze.
Why: Delicate tannins and red fruit pair beautifully with rich, gamey duck.

Mornington Peninsula
Wine: Pinot Noir
Pairing: Grilled salmon with dill butter.
Why: A perfect match—silky texture, subtle smoke, and elegant acidity.

Rutherglen

Wine: Fortified Muscat
Pairing: Sticky date pudding with butterscotch sauce.
Why: Decadent + decadent = dessert heaven. The ultimate sweet-on-sweet pairing.

New South Wales

Hunter Valley
Wine: Semillon (young or aged)
Pairing: Pan-seared scallops with brown butter.
Why: Young Semillon = citrusy zip; aged = creamy complexity. Both sing with shellfish.

Canberra District
Wine: Shiraz–Viognier blend
Pairing: Five-spice pork belly.
Why: Floral lift from Viognier pairs with aromatic spice; supple tannins pair well with pork fat.

Orange
Wine: Chardonnay
Pairing: Chicken with creamy mushroom sauce.
Why: Cool-climate Chardonnay strikes a balance between richness, freshness, and finesse.

Western Australia

Margaret River
Wine: Cabernet Sauvignon
Pairing: Herb-crusted rack of lamb.
Why: Elegant structure + herbal lift = a match made for fine dining.

Great Southern
Wine: Riesling or Pinot Noir
Pairing: Beetroot and goat cheese tart.
Why: Earthy-sweet beets + tangy cheese = magic with crisp whites or silky reds.

Tasmania

Wine: Sparkling wine or Pinot Noir
Pairing: Grilled Tasmanian oysters with lemon herb butter.
Why: Sparkling refreshes, Pinot embraces brine.
Either way, it's coastal perfection.

65

Pairing Cheat Sheet:

Wine Style	Perfect Pairing
Bold Red (Shiraz)	Grilled or roasted red meat
Cool Pinot Noir	Salmon, duck, mushrooms
Dry Riesling	Spicy Thai, Vietnamese, or oysters
Sparkling	Oysters, fried chicken, cheese boards
Semillon (Hunter)	Scallops, lemony seafood, aged cheese
Fortified Muscat	Sticky date pudding, aged blue cheese

Wine Style	Perfect Pairing
Chardonnay	Roast chicken, creamy pasta, and brie
Cabernet Sauvignon	Lamb, rosemary beef, hard aged cheese

66

New Zealand

67

North Island

Hawke's Bay

Famous For: Bordeaux-style Reds (Merlot, Cabernet), Syrah
Think: Black plum, tobacco leaf, and volcanic spice.
New Zealand's oldest wine region, with winemaking dating back to the 1850s, is located here.
Fun Fact: The **Gimblett Gravels** subregion is so famous, it's trademarked! It's a stony old riverbed that makes top-tier reds.

Top Hawke's Bay **wine producers** include Te Mata Estate, known for its iconic Coleraine blend, and Trinity Hill Wines, celebrated for its Syrah and Bordeaux-style reds. Other prominent wineries are Mission Estate Winery, Black Barn Vineyards, and Elephant Hill. These producers are part of New Zealand's oldest and second-largest wine region, which is particularly famous for its Syrah, Chardonnay, and Merlot Cabernet blends

Gisborne

Famous For: Chardonnay
Think: Pineapple, white peach, and sunny brunch wines. Known as the "Chardonnay capital" of New Zealand, Gisborne has a laid-back surf-and-sip culture.
Fun Fact: It's the first place in the world to see **the sunrise**— drink your morning mimosa in style.

Top Gisborne chardonnay producers include Villa Maria, known for its single-vineyard wines like the 'McDiarmid Hill,' Matawhero, which offers both single-vineyard and barrel-fermented chardonnays, and Millton, recognized for its organic and biodynamic approach, with the Clos de Ste. Anne Naboth's Vineyard being a standout. Other notable producers include Spade Oak, Invivo, Wrights Vineyard & Winery, and Moana Park, many of which focus on classic, tropical, and creamy chardonnay styles.

Wairarapa / Martinborough

Famous For: Pinot Noir
Think: Red cherry, forest floor, and tea leaf.
Tiny but mighty, Martinborough is renowned for its Burgundian-style Pinots, characterized by elegance and structure.
Fun Fact: Only about **1% of NZ's wine** comes from Wairarapa, but it's some of the most collectible.

Frequently recommended wineries:

Palliser Estate: Often cited as a top winery, known for its quality wines and tasting experiences.
Ata Rangi: A highly-regarded winery, consistently named a top choice for wine and cellar door visits.
Margrain Vineyard: A popular choice that appears on many lists for its wine and overall visitor experience.
Poppies: Frequently mentioned as a top winery to visit, praised for its cellar door experience.
Schubert: Another winery that is consistently recommended for its quality wine and tasting options.

Tirohana Estate: Included in several guides as a top winery in the area.
Moy Hall: A recommended option for those looking for a cellar door experience.

68

South Island

Marlborough

Famous For: Sauvignon Blanc
Think: Passionfruit, gooseberry, and electric lime.
This region put New Zealand on the global wine map in the 1980s with its explosive, zesty Sauvignon Blanc.
Fun Fact: Marlborough produces **over 70% of New Zealand's** total wine and nearly 90% of its Sauvignon Blanc. Ever heard of Cloudy Bay!?!

Popular wineries:
Cloudy Bay: One of the most famous and well-known wineries in New Zealand, particularly for its Sauvignon Blanc.
Villa Maria: Offers a wide range of wines across different tiers, from everyday wines to their prestigious Icon and Single Vineyard collections.

Hunter's Winery: Featured on many winery tours, known for its diverse selection of wines, including Sauvignon Blanc and Pinot Noir.

Allan Scott Family Winemakers: A family-owned winery that hosts events and participates in various wine showcases.

Nautilus Estate: Another popular destination for wine tasting in the region.

Central Otago

Famous For: Pinot Noir
Think: Cherries, violets, and alpine spice.
The world's southernmost commercial wine region, Central Otago, is characterized by dramatic peaks, crystal-clear lakes, and Pinot perfection.
Fun Fact: **Pinot here is more intense than in Burgundy**— sunshine and altitude do that. Additionally, winemakers often enjoy skiing before harvest.

Central Otago's top wine producers are defined by their world- class Pinot Noir, with many vineyards pioneering the region's modern wine industry, such as the oldest commercial Pinot Noir producer, Gibbston Valley Winery. This is New Zealand's premier Pinot Noir region, its growers are recognized globally, and the area is home to New Zealand's largest wine cave, at Gibbston Valley Winery. The region's producers are also known for sustainable practices, with some vineyards like Carrick Winery & Restaurant being certified organic and sustainable.

Nelson

Famous For: Aromatic Whites (Riesling, Gewürztraminer, Chardonnay.
Think: Stone fruits, ginger, and orchard blossoms.
A small, sunny region next to Marlborough, but with a more artisanal, boutique vibe.
Fun Fact: Nelson gets more **sunshine** hours than anywhere else in New Zealand—perfect for ripening grapes and creativity. Known for aromatic varieties like Sauvignon Blanc, Chardonnay, Pinot Noir, and Riesling. The area's sunny climate and varied soils, including the Moutere Hills with its clay-rich soil, produce elegant and complex wines. Nelson is New Zealand's sixth-largest wine region and a popular destination with high-quality wineries, often featuring smaller, family-owned operations.

North Canterbury / Waipara Valley

Famous For: Riesling, Pinot Noir
Think: Lime peel, beeswax, and gentle earthiness.
This under-the-radar region makes some of New Zealand's best Riesling, from dry to sweet.
Fun Fact: **The "Waipara wind"** cools vineyards in the afternoon, locking in acidity and making these wines age beautifully.

Notable producers and styles:
Bell Hill: A highly-regarded winery known for its precise, complex, and concentrated Pinot Noir wines. It has a cult following and is farmed organically and biodynamically.
Pyramid Valley: Another producer that is farmed organically and biodynamically. Its wines are often described as wild and soulful, with a strong emphasis on vineyard-specific character. **Greystone:** This winery has transitioned to organic viticulture, with its entire 33-hectare vineyard certified organic. It has also begun exploring regenerative practices, planting flowers and crops between the vine rows.

Crater Rim: One of the larger producers in North Canterbury, this winery is moving towards organic certification and launched a sparkling wine program in 2016.
Waipara Springs: An established winery that offers tastings and is known for producing high-quality wines from the region.

69

Cheat Sheet- New Zealand Wine by Style & Region

Wine Style	Go Here
Zesty, iconic whites	Marlborough
Bold alpine Pinot Noir	Central Otago
Elegant Pinot & Riesling	Martinborough, Waipara
Big reds & Syrah	Hawke's Bay
Sunny Chardonnay	Gisborne
Aromatic boutique whites	Nelson

70

New Zealand Wine & Food Pairings by Region

Marlborough

Wine: Sauvignon Blanc
Pairing: Green-lipped mussels with lemon + herbs. Why it works: Zesty, high-acid Sauv Blanc is like a squeeze of citrus—perfect with briny shellfish.
Also try: Goat cheese salad, Thai green curry.

Central Otago

Wine: Pinot Noir
Pairing: Duck breast with cherry compote. Why it works: Elegant Pinot + rich duck = a classic love story.
Also try: Lamb chops, mushroom risotto.

Nelson

Wine: Aromatic Whites (Riesling, Gewürztraminer)
Pairing: Vietnamese spring rolls with sweet chili sauce.
Why it works: Fragrant wines pair well with fresh herbs and spices.
Also try: Ginger pork, sushi, and spiced roasted carrots.

North Canterbury / Waipara

Wine: Riesling (dry to off-dry)
Pairing: Spicy Sichuan chicken or Thai papaya salad.
Why it works: Riesling's acidity and touch of sweetness cool down the heat beautifully.
Also try: Indian biryani, pork belly.

Hawke's Bay

Wine: Bordeaux Blends (Merlot, Cab), Syrah
Pairing: Chargrilled steak with rosemary and garlic.
Why it works: Bold tannins pair well with fat and savory herbs.
Also try: Beef stew, blue cheese, and smoky BBQ.

Gisborne

Wine: Chardonnay
Pairing: Grilled snapper with citrus butter.
Why it works: The round, fruity Chardonnay pairs well with bright flavors like fish and lemon.
Also try: Corn chowder, roast chicken, creamy pasta.

Wairarapa / Martinborough

Wine: Pinot Noir
Pairing: Venison with blackberry glaze.
Why it works: Gamey meats paired with structured Pinot creates complexity upon complexity.
Also try: Duck confit, lentil stew, beetroot salad.

71

Bonus: Pairing Guide by Wine Style

Wine Style	Pairing Ideas
Sauvignon Blanc	Shellfish, goat cheese, Thai food
Pinot Noir	Duck, lamb, mushrooms, and game meats
Riesling (dry/off-dry)	Spicy Asian, pork, and Indian curries
Chardonnay	Roast chicken, fish, creamy pastas
Bordeaux-style blends	Steak, aged cheddar, grilled sausages
Syrah	BBQ ribs, charcuterie, and lamb tagine
Gewürztraminer	Indian food, pad Thai, and pumpkin dishes

72

South Africa

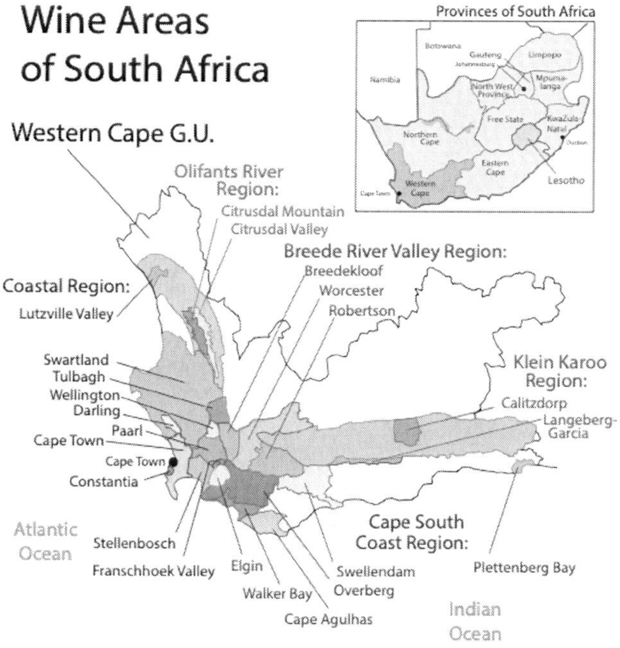

Copyright: Society of Wine Educators 2020

73

South Africa's Wine Regions

Stellenbosch

Signature Grapes: Cabernet Sauvignon, Merlot, Chenin Blanc, Sauvignon Blanc **Established:** 1679 – One of South Africa's oldest towns Fun Fact: Stellenbosch is home to South Africa's **first wine route**, founded in 1971—it now boasts over 150 wineries.

Top Stellenbosch wine producers are known for their high- quality Cabernet Sauvignon, Chenin Blanc, and Bordeaux-style blends, with many historical estates dating back to the 17th century. Key players include the historic estates like Meerlust and Rustenburg, and contemporary leaders such as Stellenbosch Vineyards, Le Riche, and boutique wineries that are defining the region's identity. The region is also recognized for its role in education through the University of Stellenbosch and pioneering wine tourism.

Constantia

Signature Grapes: Sauvignon Blanc, Muscat, Semillon
Established: 1685 (by Simon van der Stel
Fun Fact: Constantia was the source of **Napoleon's favorite sweet wine, the legendary Vin de Constance**.

The top Constantia wine producers include Groot Constantia, South Africa's oldest wine estate (founded 1685), and Klein Constantia, known for its historic vineyards and sweet dessert wine, Vin de Constance. Other key players are the historic Steenberg Estate, which features a five-star hotel and restaurant, and boutique estate Constantia Glen, which has gained a reputation for its bespoke wines.

Paarl

Signature Grapes: Shiraz, Chenin Blanc, Pinotage
Fun Fact: The town of Paarl was once home to KWV, one of the largest co-ops in the Southern Hemisphere— essential in shaping the modern industry.

The name "Paarl" is Dutch for "pearl," referring to the large granite rock on Paarl Mountain that appears like a pearl after it rains. French Huguenots were granted land in the area in the 1680s, establishing viticulture.
Pioneering innovations: The region is credited with several "firsts" in South African winemaking, including:
The country's first Viognier bottling.
The country's first Bordeaux blend.
The world's first white Pinotage.
The world's first Pinotage fortified dessert wine.

Franschhoek

Signature Grapes: Semillon, Cabernet Sauvignon, Chardonnay **Fun Fact:** "Franschhoek" means "French Corner" in Dutch— named after Huguenot settlers who brought their winemaking traditions in the late 1600s.
Highlight: Although small, it boasts a strong food and wine tourism scene and produces some of the finest Semillon in the Southern Hemisphere, often blended with Sauvignon Blanc.

Key producers:
La Bri: One of the oldest farms, focusing on expressing the unique terroir with estate-grown grapes, particularly a well- regarded Cabernet Sauvignon and Chardonnay.
Glenwood Vineyards: Known for its award-winning Chardonnay and its unique "Wine and Sushi Experience," a creative pairing that highlights the region's culinary excellence.
Colmant: The first wine farm in South Africa dedicated exclusively to producing Méthode Cap Classique (MCC) sparkling wine, making it a must-visit for sparkling wine enthusiasts.
Stony Brook Vineyards: A family-run boutique winery that combines old-world winemaking traditions with a modern spirit, producing acclaimed wines from grapes like Cabernet Sauvignon and Semillon.
Black Elephant Vintners (BEV): An innovative producer that connects wine and music through unique tasting experiences like "silent discos," highlighting the joyful and creative side of winemaking.

Swartland

Signature Grapes: Chenin Blanc, Syrah, Grenache, Cinsault **Fun Fact:** Swartland is South Africa's hub for natural wine, dry farming, and minimal intervention winemaking.

Highlight: Once overlooked, Swartland now leads the "New South African wine revolution," with old bush vines yielding concentrated, textural wines from decomposed granite and shale soils.

Top Swartland **wine producers** include Mullineux & Leeu, awarded "Winery of the Year" multiple times, and Sadie Family Wines, known for its innovative and terroir-focused approach. Lammershoek is noted for its long history, minimal intervention wines, and position as an early farm in the region, while Allesverloren is famous for its port-style wines.

Walker Bay (Hemel-en-Aarde)

Signature Grapes: Pinot Noir, Chardonnay
Fun Fact: "Hemel-en-Aarde" translates to "Heaven and Earth"— a poetic name for this cool-climate paradise.
Highlight: Close to the Atlantic, this is **South Africa's answer to Burgundy:** elegant Pinot Noir and mineral-driven Chardonnay grown in sea-breezed vineyards with ancient clay and iron-rich soils.

Key producers and their contributions:
Hamilton Russell Vineyards: Considered a pioneer in the region, Tim Hamilton Russell acquired the land and planted the first vineyards in 1975, which was a pivotal moment for establishing the area's potential for cool-climate wines.
Storm Wines: Winemaker Hannes Storm crafts wines from all three wards of the Hemel-en-Aarde region, focusing on the distinct characteristics of each. His wines are known for their minimal intervention approach, showcasing the potential of the region as the vines mature.
Newton Johnson: A highly-regarded winery in the region, Newton Johnson is recognized as one of the many boutique estates that contribute to the area's reputation for producing fine and sought-after wines.

Elgin

Signature Grapes: Sauvignon Blanc, Chardonnay, Pinot Noir
Fun Fact: Once known for apples, Elgin is now one of South Africa's coolest wine-growing areas, perfect for crisp, aromatic whites.

Top **wine producers** in the Elgin region of South Africa include Paul Clüver Family Wines, Iona Wines, and Oak Valley Estate. Other highly regarded producers are Almenkerk Wine Estate, Charles Fox Cap Classique Wine Estate, and Elgin Ridge. For producers in the Elgin, Arizona area, consider Callaghan Vineyards, Flying Leap Vineyards & Distillery, and Kief-Joshua Vineyards.

Breede River Valley (including Robertson & Worcester)

Signature Grapes: Chardonnay, Shiraz, Colombar
Fun Fact: The Robertson Wine Valley is known as the "Valley of Wine and Roses" and produces some of South Africa's top Cap Classique (sparkling) wines.
Highlight: Warm days and limestone-rich soils produce lush yet structured whites and value-driven reds; also a major source of base wine for sparkling production.

Prominent Wine Producers:
Graham Beck: An acclaimed producer of top-quality sparkling wines made using the method cap classique.

Springfield Estate: Located in the Robertson sub-region, it is celebrated for its minimal intervention winemaking, especially its Chenin Blanc and Shiraz.
Bon Courage: An established winery in Robertson, known for producing a variety of high-quality wines, including Chenin Blanc, Chardonnay, and sparkling wines.
Viljoensdrift: Situated along the Breede River, this estate is known for its wines like Cabernet Sauvignon and offers wine tastings, boat cruises, and picnics.
De Wetshof: With a long winemaking history, this Robertson winery is renowned for its Chardonnay and Cabernet Sauvignon.
Tanagra Wine Estate: An idyllic farm located near McGregor that is part of the Robertson Wine Route.

Olifants River & Citrusdal Mountain

Signature Grapes: Colombar, Chenin Blanc
Fun Fact: Some of the oldest Chenin vines in South Africa— dating back to the 1880s—can be found here.
Highlight: Hot and arid, but cooled by altitude and ocean influence, these regions are

key for bulk wine but also emerging as sources of heritage vine revival.
Top **wine producers** in the Olifants River and Citrusdal Mountain region include Namaqua Wines, Klawer Cellars, Piekenierskloof Wines, and boutique estates like Sumaridge and Tierhoek. These wineries are known for a range of wines that reflect the region's diverse terroir, from value-driven options to premium offerings from the mountainous areas.

74

South Africa Cheat Sheet

Region	Known For
Stellenbosch	Structured reds & elegant whites
Constantia	Cool-climate Sauvignon & sweet wine
Paarl	Rich reds, warmer climate
Franschhoek	Food & wine tourism, Semillon
Swartland	Natural wine & old bush vines
Walker Bay	Cool-climate Pinot & Chardonnay
Elgin	Crisp whites, high elevation
Breede River Valley	Sparkling, value wines
Olifants/Citrusdal	Bulk wine + old vines

75

South Africa Wine & Food Pairings by Region

Stellenbosch

Wine: Cabernet Sauvignon, Merlot, Chenin Blanc
Pairing: Karoo lamb chops with rosemary & garlic.
Cabernet's structure complements grilled meats.
Chenin offers a fresh counterpoint to rich textures.

Constantia

Wine: Sauvignon Blanc, Vin de Constance (sweet Muscat)
Pairing: Cape Malay chicken curry or spiced yellowtail.
Sauvignon cuts through spice beautifully.
Vin de Constance shines with aromatic desserts or blue cheese.

Paarl

Wine: Shiraz, Pinotage, Chenin Blanc
Pairing: Boerewors (South African sausage) with pap and chakalaka.
Shiraz handles smoky spices.
Pinotage loves the rich umami of grilled sausage.

Franschhoek

Wine: Semillon, Cabernet Sauvignon, Chardonnay
Pairing: Butter chicken with roti.
Semillon's texture and acidity balance creamy spice.
Chardonnay pairs well with richer sauces and fish curries.

Swartland

Wine: Old-vine Chenin Blanc, Syrah, Grenache
Pairing: Braai-roasted peri-peri chicken or vegetable bobotie.
Chenin handles heat and complexity.
Syrah adds smoky, peppery synergy with grilled meats.

Walker Bay / Hemel-en-Aarde

Wine: Pinot Noir, Chardonnay
Pairing: Grilled line fish or mussels in white wine broth with Chardonnay and seafood is a classic combination.
Pinot Noir pairs well with richer shellfish or mushroom risotto.

Elgin

Wine: Sauvignon Blanc, Chardonnay, Pinot Noir
Pairing: Springbok carpaccio with rocket and parmesan.
High-acid whites or light reds complement lean game meats and fresh, herbaceous notes.

Breede River Valley (Robertson & Worcester)

Wine: Chardonnay, Shiraz, Cap Classique
Pairing: Smoked trout pâté or chicken liver parfait.
Chardonnay and sparkling pair beautifully with creamy textures.
Shiraz works with peppered meats.

Olifants River / Citrusdal Mountain

Wine: Colombar, Chenin Blanc
Pairing: Cape snoek braai with apricot jam glaze.
These aromatic whites lift the sweet-savory fish glaze and enhance
flame-grilled flavors.

76

Quick Pairing Table

Region	Wine Style	Food Pairing
Stellenbosch	Bold reds, crisp Chenin	Karoo lamb, grilled vegetables
Constantia	Zesty whites, sweet Muscat	Cape Malay curry, blue cheese, baklava
Paarl	Spicy reds, Chenin	Boerewors, chakalaka, braaied meats
Franschhoek	Semillon, Chardonnay, Cab	Butter chicken, creamy seafood, roti
Swartland	Natural Chenin, Syrah	Peri-peri chicken, lentil bobotie

Region	Wine Style	Food Pairing
Walker Bay	Pinot Noir, Chardonnay	Grilled linefish, mussels, mushroom risotto
Elgin	Cool-climate whites, Pinot Noir	Springbok, trout, green veggies
Breede River Valley	Sparkling, Chardonnay, Shiraz	Chicken liver pâté, trout, cheeses
Olifants River	Colombar, Chenin Blanc	Snoek braai with apricot glaze

77

The United States- California

78

California Wine Regions

Napa Valley

Known For: Cabernet Sauvignon, Merlot, Chardonnay
Sub-AVAs: Rutherford, Oakville, Stags Leap, Carneros, and Howell Mountain. Napa is California's most prestigious wine region. Its Mediterranean climate, varied elevations, and well-drained soils allow world-class Bordeaux-style wines to thrive.
Fun Fact: Despite its fame, **Napa produces only 4% of California's total wine** volume, but it generates a third of its wine revenue due to premium pricing.

Highly-acclaimed producers:

Stags Leap Wine Cellars: Famous for winning the "Judgment of Paris" tasting in 1976, making a name for itself with its Cabernet Sauvignon.

Hyde Vineyards: While Hyde Vineyards is in Napa Valley, not Sonoma, many top Sonoma producers source grapes from it for their award-winning wines, making it a "top Sonoma vineyard" in terms of influence. Key Sonoma wineries that use Hyde Vineyard fruit include Kistler Vineyards, Patz & Hall, Aubert, and Paul Hobbs, who are known for their high-scoring Chardonnay and Pinot Noir.

Chateau Montelena: Another winery that gained fame from the 1976 tasting with its Chardonnay.

Far Niente Winery: Known for its elegant and age-worthy Napa Valley Cabernet Sauvignon.

Sonoma County

Known For: Pinot Noir, Chardonnay, Zinfandel

Sub-AVAs: Russian River Valley, Sonoma Coast, Dry Creek, Alexander Valley, and Carneros.

Sonoma spans over 1 million acres and offers a diverse array of microclimates. Cool zones like the Russian River are ideal for Pinot Noir and Chardonnay, while Dry Creek and Alexander Valley produce rich Zinfandel and Cabernet.

Fun Fact: Sonoma has more AVAs (18!) than any other California county, showcasing just how regionally expressive its wines can be.

Gary Farrell Vineyards: A highly-rated winery, especially known for its Russian River Valley Pinot Noir and Chardonnay.

Peter Michael Winery: Known for its high-end, world-class wines.

William Selyem Winery: A historically significant producer, particularly for its Pinot Noir and Zinfandel.

Merry Edwards Winery: Celebrated for its high-quality wines and the expertise of its winemakers.

Gloria Ferrer Caves & Vineyards: Famous for its sparkling wines.
J Vineyards & Winery: Known for its sparkling wines and Chardonnays.
Dutton-Goldfield Winery: A winery that produces high-quality wines, particularly known for its Chardonnay and Pinot Noir.
Peay Vineyards: A well-regarded producer located on the Sonoma Coast.

Paso Robles

Known For: Rhône-style blends, Zinfandel, Cabernet Sauvignon **Sub-AVAs:** Adelaida District, Willow Creek, Templeton Gap Paso Robles is one of California's most innovative regions. It's warm days and cool nights support bold reds and eclectic blends. The area is also a hub for sustainable and dry-farmed vineyards.
Fun Fact: Paso is home to the largest AVA in California by area, and some vineyards experience diurnal swings of up to 50°F—ideal for preserving acidity in robust reds. Some top Paso Robles wine producers include Daou Vineyards, known for its Cabernet Sauvignon, and established wineries like Eberle Winery and JUSTIN Vineyards & Winery. Other highly regarded producers are Tablas Creek Vineyard, Halter Ranch, and

those focusing on Rhône and Bordeaux-style blends like Law Estate Wines and Booker Wines.

Santa Barbara County

Known For: Pinot Noir, Chardonnay, Syrah
Sub-AVAs: Sta. Rita Hills, Santa Maria Valley, Santa Ynez Valley Santa Barbara's transverse valleys (running east-west) pull in cool Pacific air, making it one of California's best zones for elegant, cool-climate wines. Coastal zones produce expressive Pinot Noir and Chardonnay, while inland areas favor Rhône and Bordeaux varieties.
Fun Fact: Sideways, the 2004 wine movie filmed in Santa Barbara, helped boost Pinot Noir sales worldwide and caused a notable drop in Merlot consumption!

Top wine producers:

Sanford Winery: A historic and well-regarded winery, particularly known for its Pinot Noir and Chardonnay from its La Rinconada and Sanford & Benedict vineyards.

Stolpman Vineyards: Celebrated for its wines, including Syrah, with a tasting room in Los Olivos.
Grassini Family Vineyards: Based in the Happy Canyon appellation, they are recognized for producing high-quality Sauvignon Blanc and other wines.
Melville Winery: Known for its estate-grown Pinot Noir and Chardonnay from the Sta. Rita Hills region.
Au Bon Climat: A long-standing producer recognized for elegant Pinot Noir and Chardonnay.

Central Coast (Broad AVA)

Known For: Albariño, Chardonnay, Syrah, Pinot Noir **Includes:** Monterey, San Luis Obispo, Santa Lucia Highlands. This sprawling AVA includes diverse subregions, from foggy coastal vineyards to sunny hillsides. Monterey County excels at ocean-cooled whites, while Edna Valley and Santa Lucia Highlands are known for their site-specific, artisanal production.
Fun Fact: Central Coast is a hotbed for alternative varieties— expect to see Grüner Veltliner, Vermentino, and Tempranillo thriving here.

Bernardus Winery: Located in Carmel Valley, is known for its estate vineyards and award-winning wines.
Folktale Winery & Vineyard: Situated in Carmel Valley, this is a popular stop for wine tasting.
Chalone Vineyard: A historic winery known for its estate-grown wines.
Wrath Wines: Features a Carmel-by-the-Sea tasting room and produces site-driven wines like Pinot Noir and Chardonnay from its own estate vineyards.

Scheid Vineyards: Family-owned with vineyards across the Salinas Valley, benefiting from diverse microclimates.
Talbott Vineyards: A well-established winery known for high-quality Chardonnay from its Sleepy Hollow Vineyard.

Lodi

Known For: Old Vine Zinfandel, Tempranillo, Petite Sirah
Sub-AVAs: Mokelumne River, Clements Hills, Borden Ranch. Located between the Sierra Foothills and the Delta, Lodi's deep sandy soils and warm days create ripe, fruit-forward reds. It's primarily known for its heritage vines, which were planted in the early 20th century.
Fun Fact: Lodi is home to more old-vine Zinfandel than anywhere else in the world, with some vineyards planted in the 1880s still producing today.

Some of the top Lodi wine producers include Harney Lane Vineyards, Klinker Brick Winery, Oak Farm Vineyards, Jessie's Grove Winery, and Oak Ridge Winery. Other notable producers are m2 Wines, Acquiesce

Winery, and Bokisch Vineyards, which focus on diverse varietals, including Lodi's renowned old-vine Zinfandel.

Mendocino County

Known For: Pinot Noir, Gewürztraminer, Chardonnay
Sub-AVAs: Anderson Valley, Redwood Valley, Potter Valley Mendocino is California's most eco-conscious region, with a high percentage of organic and biodynamic vineyards. Anderson Valley is renowned for its cool-climate wines, particularly sparkling and aromatic whites.
Fun Fact: Over 25% of Mendocino's vineyards are certified organic, more than any other county in the state.

Top wineries:

Husch Vineyards & Winery:
Produces 22 wines in small batches, and their 2023 Late Harvest Gewürztraminer and 2023 Sauvignon Blanc won top honors at the 2024 Mendocino Wine Competition. Other top offerings include Chardonnay and Pinot Noir. The oldest winery in Anderson Valley, Husch

operates out of a converted pony barn from the early 1900s.

Navarro Vineyards & Winery:

Wines: Known for its fresh and elegant Alsatian-style white wines, including Gewürztraminer, Riesling, and Muscat Blanc. Their Pinot Noir and Chardonnay are also highly regarded.

Goldeneye Winery:

Part of the Duckhorn family, Goldeneye is considered a top producer of Pinot Noir in the Anderson Valley.

Accolades: Mendocino County, where Goldeneye is based, was named the "2024 American Wine Region of the Year" by Wine Enthusiast.

Sierra Foothills

Known For: Zinfandel, Barbera, Syrah
Sub-AVAs: El Dorado, Amador, Calaveras
This historic region dates back to California's Gold Rush. Its elevation, granite soils, and heritage vines yield bold, rustic reds with depth and personality. It's also an exciting frontier for winemakers working with forgotten European varietals.
Fun Fact: The Sierra Foothills AVA includes vineyards over 150 years old, and many are dry farmed, meaning no irrigation is used at all.

Notable Sierra Valley and foothill producers:
Andis Winery: Known for modern winemaking in the historic Shenandoah Valley.
Lucchesi Vineyards & Winery: Specializes in small-batch, traditionally crafted wines.
Miramont Estate Vineyards: A premier estate winery in the Sierra Nevada foothills, with over 80 awards for its wines.

79

Summary Chart: California Regions + Highlights

Region	Signature Grapes	Highlights
Napa Valley	Cabernet Sauvignon, Merlot	Produces 4% of CA wine, but dominates premium sales
Sonoma County	Pinot Noir, Chardonnay, Zinfandel	Home to 18 AVAs and coastal Pinot powerhouses
Paso Robles	Syrah, Zinfandel, GSM blends	Hottest diurnal swings + largest AVA by land area
Santa Barbara	Pinot Noir, Chardonnay, Syrah	Transverse valleys = ideal cool-climate Pinot

		conditions
Region	Signature Grapes	Highlights
Central Coast	Albariño, Syrah, Chardonnay	Experimental hotspot for offbeat grapes
Lodi	Zinfandel, Tempranillo	World's largest concentration of old-vine Zinfandel
Mendocino County	Gewürztraminer, Pinot Noir	The highest % of organic vineyards in California
Sierra Foothills	Barbera, Zinfandel, Syrah	Winegrowing dates back to the 1850s Gold Rush era

80

California Wine & Food Pairing Guide

Napa Valley

Famous For: Cabernet Sauvignon
Pair It With: Grilled ribeye, rosemary lamb, or aged cheddar.
Why It Works: Napa Cab has power, tannin, and richness— perfect for bold proteins and umami-rich bites.
Bonus Grape: Merlot — smooth, plush, and an excellent match for roast duck or mushroom risotto.

Sonoma County

Famous For: Pinot Noir & Chardonnay
Pair Pinot With: Roast chicken, salmon, or mushroom dishes.
Pair Chardonnay With: Shrimp scampi, lemon chicken, or creamy pastas.

Why It Works: Sonoma Pinot = silky and savory.
Cool-climate Chard =zippy and fresh. They're food lovers' wines.
Zinfandel Alert: In Dry Creek, try it with BBQ ribs or spicy sausage.

Paso Robles

Famous For: Rhône-style reds (Syrah, Grenache), Zinfandel
Pair It With: Short ribs, grilled lamb, burgers with blue cheese.
Why It Works: Paso reds are big, ripe, and spicy.
They love smoke, char, and richness.
Zin Tip: Pair old-vine Zinfandel with a tri-tip BBQ sandwich or pepperoni pizza.

Santa Barbara County

Famous For: Pinot Noir, Chardonnay, Syrah
Pinot Pairing: Pork tenderloin, roast duck, or tuna
Chard Pairing: Crab cakes, roast chicken, creamy risottos.
Why It Works: This is cool-climate California—elegant wines that play well with lighter meats and seafood.

Central Coast

Famous For: Variety! Albariño, Syrah, Chardonnay, Pinot
Try Albariño with: Oysters, ceviche, or goat cheese.
Try Syrah with: Grilled eggplant, lamb kebabs, or shakshuka.
Why It Works: The Central Coast is a hub of innovation.
Fresh whites, spicy reds, and room to play with food.

Lodi

Famous For: Old Vine Zinfandel
Pair It With: Pulled pork, shepherd's pie, or smoky brisket.
Why It Works: Lodi Zinfandel is fruity, spicy, and smooth— great for anything from the grill or smoker.
Bonus Grapes: Tempranillo and Barbera, perfect with grilled sausages or pizza.

Mendocino County

Famous For: Gewürztraminer, Pinot Noir
Try Gewürz With: Thai curry, Indian samosas, or spicy stir-fry.

Try Pinot with: roast veggies, duck, or baked salmon.
Why It Works: This is a territory of aromatics and elegance. Great with spice or earthy comfort food.
Fun Fact: Mendocino leads the state in organic vineyards.

Sierra Foothills

Famous For: Zinfandel, Barbera, Syrah
Zin Pairing: Smoky ribs, BBQ chicken, or chili **Barbera Pairing:** Spaghetti Bolognese or lasagna.
Why It Works: High-altitude reds = bold, rustic, and ready for hearty plates.

81

Bonus Pairing Tips by Style

Wine Style	Pairs Well With...
Bold Red (Cab, Syrah)	Grilled meats, aged cheeses, hearty stews
Lighter Red (Pinot Noir)	Roasted poultry, mushrooms, and root vegetables
Aromatic White (Gewürz)	Spicy dishes, Asian cuisine, and floral cheeses
Crisp White (Albariño)	Shellfish, citrus salads, chèvre
Full White (Chardonnay)	Rich seafood, cream sauces, roasted poultry
Zinfandel	BBQ, spice rubs, smoky or tomato-based sauces

82

Washington

83

Washington's Wine Regions

Columbia Valley

Signature Grapes: Cabernet Sauvignon, Merlot, Syrah, Chardonnay, Riesling.
Fun Fact: This AVA covers nearly 11 million acres, making it larger than the entire country of Portugal!

Renowned producers:

Chateau Ste. Michelle: One of Washington's most well-known wineries, it produces a wide range of wines, including some from the historic Cold Creek Vineyard.
Maryhill Winery: A family-owned winery recognized for its diverse and award-winning portfolio that sources grapes from across the Columbia Valley's various AVAs.
Abeja Winery: Named Washington Winery of the Year in 2023, it gained recognition for its 2019 Columbia Valley Merlot.

Dunham Cellars: A well-regarded producer, especially noted for its Chardonnay wines.
Hedges Family Estate: Another prominent producer, with its wines like CMS and House of Independent Producers Chardonnay receiving accolades.
L'Ecole No. 41: A producer that has been recognized for a variety of its wines from the region.

Walla Walla Valley AVA

Signature Grapes: Cabernet Sauvignon, Merlot, Syrah
Fun Fact: The town of Walla Walla was once known for onions, but now it's home to over 120 wineries in under 30 miles!
Highlight: The region's cobblestone vineyards mimic those of the Rhône Valley, producing Syrah with serious complexity and savory character.
Located in: Southeastern corner (extends into Oregon Known for its reputation-driven producers and diverse vineyards, Walla Walla is a subregion of the Columbia Valley.

Pioneering and established wineries:

Woodward Canyon Winery: One of the valley's founding wineries, established in 1981, known for its award-winning Cabernet Sauvignon and Chardonnay.
Seven Hills Winery: A well-regarded producer with a long history in the region.
Leonetti Cellar: Another of the earliest wineries in the area.
Modern and acclaimed wineries:
Doubleback Winery: Founded by former NFL quarterback Drew Bledsoe, this winery is known for its estate Cabernet Sauvignon and Merlot.
Long Shadows Winery: Known for its partnerships with world-renowned winemakers and for having what was named America's best wine tasting room by USA Today's Reader Choice Awards.
Echolands Winery: A newer winery focused on regenerative farming practices, using grapes from other vineyards while its estate is being developed.

Red Mountain AVA

Signature Grapes: Cabernet Sauvignon, Merlot, Syrah
Fun Fact: Despite being Washington's smallest AVA,
(~4,040 acres Red Mountain has some of the state's most expensive vineyard land per acre. Despite its name, Red Mountain is a **sun-drenched southwest-facing slope near the Yakima River**.
It's one of the warmest and driest AVAs in the state, producing intensely concentrated, structured wines with bold tannins and exceptional age-worthiness.
Kiona Vineyards and Winery: One of the oldest and most established producers, with some of the first vines planted on Red Mountain in the 1970s.
Fidélitas: A boutique winery specializing in Bordeaux varietals, using fruit exclusively from Red Mountain.
Hightower Cellars: A highly regarded producer with a strong presence on the mountain.
Hamilton Cellars: A winery that has received accolades such as "Winemaker of the Year".

Col Solare: A producer with a significant history on the mountain.
Klipsun Vineyard: While not a winery itself, Klipsun is one of the most acclaimed vineyards, and its grapes are sought after by many premium wineries, including Klipsun Vineyard's wines.
Ciel du Cheval: A significant vineyard on the mountain, with its grapes used in a wide array of premium wines.

Yakima Valley AVA

Signature Grapes: Merlot, Cabernet Sauvignon, Chardonnay, Riesling
Established: 1983 – Washington's first AVA
Highlight: Yakima is the birthplace of Washington Syrah, with plantings dating back to the 1980s.
Notable Sub-AVAs: Rattlesnake Hills, Snipes Mountain. Notable Fact: Yakima is also a significant source of Rhône varietals, such as Grenache and Viognier, thanks to its diverse microclimates.

Some top Yakima Valley wine producers include Gilbert Cellars, Treveri Cellars, and Dineen Vineyards, known for their quality and distinct offerings. Other highly-regarded wineries are Hyatt Vineyards, Two Mountain Winery, and VanArnam Vineyards, which focus on hand-crafted wines from their estate vineyards.

Horse Heaven Hills AVA

Signature Grapes: Cabernet Sauvignon, Merlot, Syrah
Fun Fact: The name "Horse Heaven Hills" was inspired when a pioneer saw wild horses grazing and declared it "horse heaven."

Highlight: Constant breezes help reduce pests and mildew, allowing some vineyards to avoid pesticides altogether.

Prominent Wineries:
Columbia Crest: The first winery in the Horse Heaven Hills AVA, it is now the third-largest wine brand in Washington. Its wines have been featured on Wine Spectator's Top 100 Wines of the Year list 16 times.
Mercer Wine: Mercer is a family-owned winery that started producing wine in 2005 after decades of farming in the area. They produce wine under several labels and have received recognition for their wines.
Matthews Winery: This winery produces a Bordeaux-style blend and a Cuvée using grapes from the Horse Heaven Hills AVA.
Horse Heaven Wine Company: This is a producer located in the heart of the Horse Heaven Hills AVA. Cooper's Hawk: A brand that produces wine from the Horse Heaven Hills region.

Lake Chelan AVA

Signature Grapes: Syrah, Pinot Noir, Chardonnay, Riesling

Fun Fact: Lake Chelan was carved by glaciers during the Ice Age and helps regulate vineyard temperatures, reducing frost risk. Highlight: It's a top destination for wine tourism, thanks to scenic lake views, charming tasting rooms, and a growing food scene.

Some of the top Lake Chelan wine producers include Tsillan Cellars, known for its Italian-style estate and small-lot wines, Karma Vineyards, recognized for its sparkling wines, and Benson Vineyards Estate Winery, a family-owned winery famous for its port-style wines. Other notable wineries in the region are Cairdeas Winery, Wapato Point Cellars, and Amos Rome Vineyards.

Ancient Lakes of Columbia Valley AVA

Signature Grapes: Riesling, Chardonnay, Pinot Gris
Fun Fact: The soils here are the result of cataclysmic Ice Age floods, leaving behind ancient limestone and gravel that are ideal for producing white wines.
Highlight: This AVA is renowned for its crisp, mineral-driven Rieslings.

Producers in the Ancient Lakes AVA:
Cave B Estate Winery: Sources 100% of its grapes from its own vineyards in the Ancient Lakes AVA and produces a wide variety of wines, including sparkling, red, and white options.
Caliche Estate: This winery focuses on premium, single-vineyard white wines, such as Albariño and Sauvignon Blanc, from the Evergreen Vineyard.
Rattlesnake Hills AVA
Signature Grapes: Merlot, Cabernet Sauvignon, Syrah, Riesling
Fun Fact: Some vineyards here reach over 3,000 feet in elevation, among the highest in the state. Highlight: Its varied terrain allows for the cultivation of both warm- and cool-climate grapes, often planted within a few miles of each other.

Prominent wine producers:

Dineen Vineyards: A key player focused on promoting the region as a premier grape-growing and wine-producing area, according to Wine Business.

Hyatt Vineyards: Known for wines like its Chardonnay and Riesling, as noted on Appellation America.

Portteus Winery: A well-regarded producer in the area.

Silver Lake Winery: Recognized for its Chenin Blanc, Gewurztraminer, and Sauvignon Blanc. **Bonair Winery:** A winery on the Rattlesnake Hills Wine Trail that produces Gewurztraminer.

Horizon's Edge Winery: Also known as Horizon's Edge/Maison de Padgett Winery, it is part of the Rattlesnake Hills Wine Trail.

84

Summary Table: Washington State Wine Regions

Region	Known For	Signature Grapes
Columbia Valley	State backbone AVA	Cab, Chardonnay
Walla Walla Valley	Small-lot prestige reds	Syrah, Merlot, Cabernet
Red Mountain	Boldest reds	Cab
Yakima Valley	Old vines & diversity	Merlot, Riesling, Grenache
Horse Heaven Hills	Wind-shaped structure & depth	Bordeaux blends
Lake Chelan	Cool-climate elegance	Pinot Noir, Riesling
Ancient Lakes	Mineral-driven whites	Riesling, Chardonnay
Rattlesnake Hills	High-elevation diversity	Syrah, Cab, Riesling

85

Washington State Wine Regions with Fun Facts

Region	Fun Fact
Columbia Valley	Larger than Portugal!
Walla Walla Valley	Over 120 wineries are packed into 30 miles
Red Mountain	Smallest AVA, highest vineyard land value
Yakima Valley	Washington's first AVA (1983)
Horse Heaven Hills	Named by a horse-loving pioneer
Lake Chelan	Carved by glaciers, ideal for wine tourism
Ancient Lakes	Formed by Ice Age floods, the top spot for crisp whites
Rattlesnake Hills	Vineyards reach over 3,000 feet in elevation

86

Washington Wine & Food Pairing Guide

Columbia Valley

Wine: Cabernet Sauvignon, Merlot, Chardonnay, Riesling
Pairing Ideas:
Cabernet Sauvignon: Grilled ribeye steak with rosemary potatoes
Merlot: Roast duck with cherry reduction
Chardonnay: Dungeness crab with lemon butter
Riesling (Dry): Thai green curry or apple-glazed pork chops Why it works: Columbia Valley's long growing season gives ripe fruit and natural acidity, making these wines food-versatile.

Walla Walla Valley

Wine: Syrah, Cabernet Sauvignon, Merlot

Pairing Ideas:
Syrah: Braised lamb shank with olives and herbs
Cabernet Sauvignon: Aged cheddar burger or beef bourguignon
Merlot: Lentil and mushroom ragù with creamy polenta Why it works: Walla Walla Reds are savory and structured, making them perfect with umami-rich dishes.

Red Mountain

Wine: Cabernet Sauvignon, Merlot, Syrah
Pairing Ideas:
Cabernet Sauvignon: Dry-aged New York strip with black garlic butter
Syrah: Smoked brisket or BBQ short ribs
Merlot: Charred eggplant with tahini and pine nuts Why it works: These are bold, tannic wines—ideal for dishes with grilled, roasted, or smoky flavors.

Yakima Valley

Wine: Riesling, Grenache, Viognier, Syrah
Pairing Ideas:
Dry Riesling: Spicy Korean fried chicken or sushi

Grenache: Roasted beet and goat cheese salad **Viognier:** Lobster mac & cheese or chicken tagine

Syrah: Wild mushroom risotto with parmesan

Why it works: The diversity of grapes here allows for wide-ranging pairings—from spicy to creamy to earthy.

Horse Heaven Hills

Wine: Bordeaux blends (Cab/Merlot), Syrah

Pairing Ideas:

Bordeaux Blend: Herb-crusted lamb or mushroom-stuffed ravioli

Syrah: Charcuterie board with smoked meats and hard cheeses Why it works: Structured reds + protein = harmony.

The region's winds and elevation yield balanced, food-loving wines.

Lake Chelan

Wine: Pinot Noir, Syrah, Chardonnay

Pairing Ideas:

Pinot Noir: Cedar-planked salmon with cherry glaze

Chardonnay: Halibut with lemon caper sauce

Syrah: Moroccan lamb meatballs with couscous Why it works: The lake effect produces refined, aromatic wines that pair well with lighter meats, seafood, and herbs.

Ancient Lakes of Columbia Valley

Wine: Riesling, Chardonnay, Pinot Gris
Pairing Ideas:
Riesling (Off-dry): Spicy Vietnamese pho or grilled peaches with chèvre
Chardonnay: Roasted chicken with tarragon cream
Pinot Gris: Pacific oysters or creamy pasta primavera Why it works: The high acidity and mineral edge of These wines pair beautifully with rich or spicy dishes.

Rattlesnake Hills

Wine: Syrah, Cabernet Sauvignon, Riesling
Pairing Ideas:
Syrah: Duck breast with cherry gastrique
Cabernet Sauvignon: Stuffed portobello mushrooms
Riesling: Apple and fennel slaw with grilled sausages Why it works: A region of altitude

and diversity— great for both hearty and delicate dishes.

87

Quick Cheat Sheet: Pair by Style

Wine Style	Food Match
Bold reds (Cab/Syrah)	Grilled meats, BBQ, aged cheeses
Medium reds (Merlot)	Duck, mushrooms, root vegetables
Crisp whites (Riesling, Pinot Gris)	Spicy cuisine, seafood, and salads
Full whites (Chardonnay, Viognier)	Rich seafood, cream sauces
Lighter reds (Pinot Noir)	Salmon, poultry, and mushroom risotto

88

Oregon

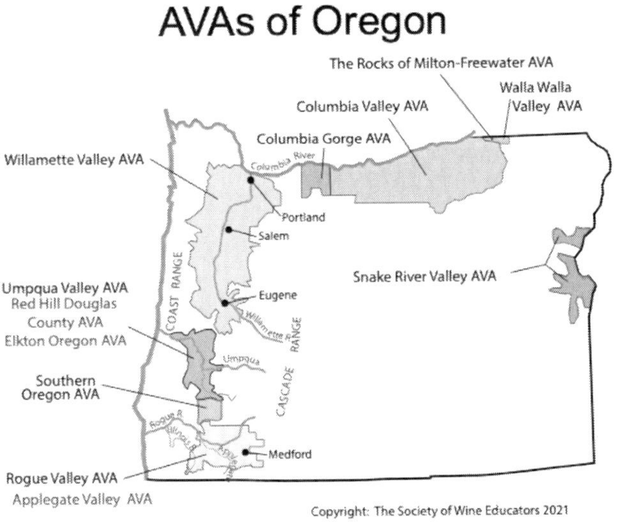
AVAs of Oregon
The Rocks of Milton-Freewater AVA
Walla Walla Valley AVA
Columbia Valley AVA
Columbia Gorge AVA
Willamette Valley AVA
Columbia River
Portland
Salem
Snake River Valley AVA
Eugene
Umpqua Valley AVA
Red Hill Douglas County AVA
Elkton Oregon AVA
COAST RANGE
Willamette R.
Umpqua
CASCADE RANGE
Southern Oregon AVA
Rogue R.
Medford
Rogue Valley AVA
Applegate Valley AVA
Copyright: The Society of Wine Educators 2021

89

Oregon's Wine Regions

Oregon may account for only about 1% of U.S. wine production. Still, its influence far exceeds its size, especially when it comes to cool-climate varietals, terroir expression, and sustainable farming practices.

Willamette Valley AVA

Signature Grapes: Pinot Noir, Chardonnay, Pinot Gris Established: 1984 Location: Northwestern Oregon, west of the Cascade Mountains

Sub-AVAs: Dundee Hills, Eola-Amity Hills, Yamhill-Carlton, Ribbon Ridge, Chehalem Mountains, McMinnville, Laurelwood District, Tualatin Hills

Established producers:

Domaine Drouhin Oregon: An Oregon outpost of a historic Burgundy house, known for its critically acclaimed Pinot Noirs and Chardonnays that express the local terroir.

Adelsheim Vineyard: One of the founding wineries of the region, Adelsheim is celebrated for its pioneering spirit and commitment to Pinot Noir and Chardonnay.
Domaine Serene: A well-known estate that produces acclaimed Pinot Noirs and Chardonnays.

The Willamette Valley is Oregon's flagship wine region, responsible for nearly 70% of the state's wine production. It's internationally acclaimed for Pinot Noir, thanks to its mild, maritime-influenced climate and diverse volcanic and sedimentary soils.
Fun Fact: Oregon's wine industry took off in the 1970s when pioneering winemakers (like David Lett of Eyrie Vineyards) proved that Pinot Noir could thrive here, earning international acclaim just decades later.

Eola-Amity Hills (Sub-AVA of Willamette Valley)

Signature Grapes: Pinot Noir, Chardonnay
Highlight: Known for brisk afternoon winds from the Van Duzer Corridor, which cools the vineyards and enhances grape acidity and tannin structure.
Fun Fact: "Eola" is named after the Greek god of winds, Aeolus— a nod to the region's daily cooling gusts.

Top **wine producers** in the Eola-Amity Hills include Cristom Vineyards, known for its single-vineyard Pinot Noirs, and Brooks Wine, which produces Pinot Noirs and Rieslings. Other highly-regarded producers in the region are Domaine Drouhin Oregon, with its Roserock Vineyard, and Bergström Wines.

Dundee Hills (Sub-AVA of Willamette Valley)

Signature Grapes: Pinot Noir
Highlight: Reddish volcanic Jory soils and a slightly warmer climate lead to richly fruited Pinots with floral and baking spice notes.
Fun Fact: This is where Oregon Pinot Noir was born, home to pioneering wineries like Domaine Drouhin, Archery Summit, and Eyrie.

Umpqua Valley AVA

Signature Grapes: Tempranillo, Syrah, Pinot Noir, Riesling
Established: 1984
Location: Southern Oregon, between the Willamette and Rogue Valleys.

Fun Fact: Oregon's first post-Prohibition winery, HillCrest Vineyard, was established here in 1961.
A transitional climate between the cooler north and warmer south, Umpqua supports both cool- and warm-climate grapes.
The region is gaining recognition for its complex, age-worthy Tempranillo and balanced Syrah.

Some top Umpqua Valley wine producers include Abacela, known for being the first to plant Tempranillo in Oregon, Hillcrest Vineyard, Oregon's oldest estate winery, and Reustle Prayer Rock Vineyards. Other notable producers are Cooper Ridge Vineyard, which has an estate with multiple grape varieties, and Melrose Vineyards.

90

Summary Table: Oregon Wine Regions with Fun Facts

Region	Known For	Fun Fact
Willamette Valley	Flagship cool-climate AVA	Produces 70%+ of Oregon's wine
Eola-Amity Hills	Wind-cooled acidity + structure	Named after the god of winds
Dundee Hills	Volcanic soils + classic Pinot sites	Birthplace of Oregon Pinot
Umpqua Valley	Transitional climate diversity	Site of Oregon's first modern winery
Rogue Valley	Warmest AVA in Oregon	Over 2,800 hours of sun annually

Region	Known For	Fun Fact
Applegate Valley	Elevation + natural winemaking	Biodynamic + organic wine hotspot
Columbia Gorge	Microclimate mosaic	"A world of wine in 40 miles"
Columbia Valley (OR)	Warmest northeastern corner	Oregon's link to WA's powerhouse reds

91

Oregon Food & Wine Pairing Guide

Willamette Valley AVA

Signature Grapes: Pinot Noir, Chardonnay, Pinot Gris, Riesling
Pairing Ideas:
Pinot Noir: Herb-crusted pork tenderloin or wild mushroom risotto
Chardonnay: Dungeness crab with lemon butter
Pinot Gris: Grilled pear salad with hazelnuts and goat cheese
Riesling (off-dry): Curry or glazed roast chicken.
Why it works: Cool-climate acidity + Oregon's seasonal, foraged ingredients = match made in heaven.

Chehalem Mountains AVA (Sub-AVA of Willamette)

Signature Grapes: Pinot Noir, Chardonnay
Pairing Ideas:
Pinot Noir: Cedar-roasted salmon or beetroot and lentil salad.
Chardonnay: Chicken with roasted chanterelles and thyme.
Why it works: Terroir-driven wines with nuance shine best with earthy, local ingredients.

Eola-Amity Hills AVA (Sub-AVA of Willamette)

Signature Grapes: Pinot Noir, Chardonnay
Pairing Ideas:
Pinot Noir: Duck confit with cherry sauce
Chardonnay: Creamy polenta with roasted vegetables.
Why it works: The region's structure and freshness demand savory, layered dishes.

Umpqua Valley AVA (Southern Oregon)

Signature Grapes: Tempranillo, Pinot Noir, Gewürztraminer
Pairing Ideas:

Tempranillo: Smoked brisket tacos or grilled lamb
Gewürztraminer: Spicy pork dumplings or Asian slaw
Pinot Noir: Roast turkey with cranberry-orange compote.
Why it works: The warmer climate produces fuller-bodied wines that pair well with bold, spice-friendly foods.

Rogue Valley AVA (Southern Oregon)

Signature Grapes: Syrah, Cabernet Sauvignon, Viognier
Pairing Ideas:
Syrah: Lamb burgers with rosemary and feta
Cabernet Sauvignon: Ribeye with chimichurri
Viognier: Lobster tail with ginger-lime butter.
Why it works: These wines possess ripeness and body, making them perfect for richly flavored dishes.

Applegate Valley AVA (Subregion of Rogue)

Signature Grapes: Zinfandel, Merlot, Malbec
Pairing Ideas:

Zinfandel: BBQ pulled pork or sausage-stuffed peppers
Malbec: Grilled portobello with chimichurri
Merlot: Baked pasta with eggplant and mozzarella.
Why it works: Bold but balanced—great with grilled vegetables or meaty mains.

Columbia Gorge AVA (Shared with Washington)

Signature Grapes: Chardonnay, Pinot Noir, Syrah, Albariño
Pairing Ideas:
Albariño: Fresh oysters or ceviche
Pinot Noir: Roast chicken with thyme and garlic
Syrah: Charred skirt steak with black olive tapenade.
Why it works: The diversity of microclimates matches a wide range of cuisine, from coastal to Mediterranean.

92

Cheat Sheet: Oregon Wine & Food Pairing

Wine Style	Try With...	Regions
Elegant Pinot Noir	Roast pork, salmon, duck, and mushroom dishes	Willamette, Eola-Amity, Chehalem
Bright, mineral Chardonnay	Crab, chicken, creamy pastas	Willamette, Columbia Gorge
Aromatic whites (Riesling, Gewürztraminer)	Spicy cuisine, pork, fruit-based sauces	Willamette, Umpqua Valley
Full-bodied reds (Tempranillo, Syrah, Malbec)	BBQ, grilled meats, eggplant	Rogue, Applegate, Umpqua
Fresh, coastal whites	Shellfish, ceviche, citrusy salads	Columbia Gorge, Willamette

93

New York

AVAs of New York State

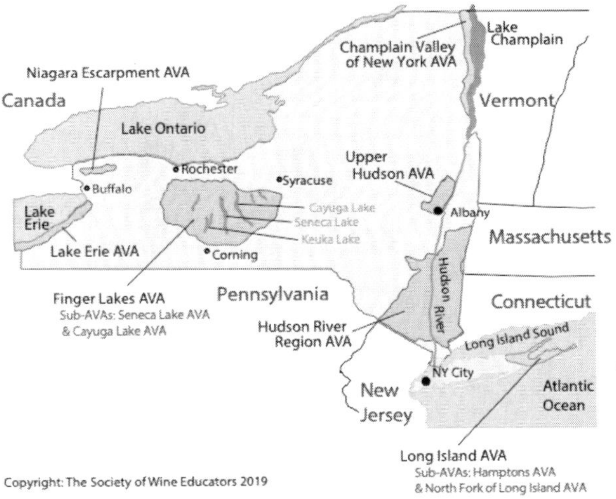

94

New York's Wine Regions

As the third-largest wine-producing state in the U.S., New York blends old-world sensibility with new-world innovation, thanks to glacial soils, calm lakes, and diverse grapes— from Riesling to Cabernet Franc.

Finger Lakes AVA

Signature Grapes: Riesling, Gewürztraminer, Cabernet Franc Established: 1982
Notable Sub-AVAs: Seneca Lake AVA, Cayuga Lake AVA
The Finger Lakes region is the heart of New York's wine industry. Deep, narrow lakes moderate the harsh winters, creating an ideal environment for aromatic whites and cool-climate reds, such as Cabernet Franc.

Top Finger Lakes **wine producers** include Dr. Konstantin Frank Winery, Ravines Wine Cellars, Hermann J. Wiemer Vineyard, and Fox Run Vineyards, which are frequently cited for their quality Riesling and cool-climate wines. Other highly- regarded wineries include Lamoreaux Landing Wine Cellars, Forge Cellars, and Wagner Vineyards, a multi-award winner and one of the region's oldest wineries.

Long Island AVA

Signature Grapes: Merlot, Cabernet Franc, Chardonnay Established: 2001 (as a broader AVA; **sub-AVAs** include North Fork and The Hamptons.

Long Island's maritime climate offers a longer growing season than Bordeaux, making it ideal for Bordeaux-style blends.

The North Fork AVA is renowned for its structured red wines and age-worthy Merlots, while the Hamptons AVA produces elegant, cooler-climate styles.

Fun Fact: Long Island has over 60 wineries packed into just 40 miles, making it a top weekend destination for NYC wine lovers.

The top Long Island wine producers, including Duck Walk, Wolffer, Channing Daughters, Pindar, and Macari, are all prominent players in the region's wine scene, known for their diverse offerings and distinct styles. Wolffer Estate, Channing Daughters, and Macari are often praised for their premium wines, while Pindar is one of the largest producers in the area, and Duck Walk is known for its wide range of varieties and popular tasting rooms.

Hudson River Region AVA

Signature Grapes: Seyval Blanc, Chardonnay, Cabernet Franc Established: 1982 Location: Along the Hudson River, north of NYC.
This historic region includes some of the oldest vineyards in the United States, which has a winemaking tradition dating back to the 1600s. The river acts as a natural temperature moderator, protecting vines from frost and supporting the hybrid varieties that thrive in the cool climate.
Fun Fact: Home to Brotherhood Winery, founded in 1839— The oldest operating winery in America.

Top Hudson Valley wine producers include Milea Estate Vineyard, which has been named "Best Winery" by Hudson Valley Magazine readers, Millbrook Vineyards & Winery, called the "flagship winery" by The New York Times, and Whitecliff Vineyard & Winery, recognized for its award-winning wines and scenic views. Other notable producers are Benmarl Winery, the first farm winery licensed in New York; Brotherhood Winery, America's oldest continuously operating winery; and Warwick Valley Winery, Distillery & Orchard, known for its unique wines, ciders, and brandies.

Lake Erie AVA

Signature Grapes: Concord, Niagara, Chambourcin, Riesling Established: 1983 Location: Western NY, stretching into Pennsylvania and Ohio
Fun Fact: The Lake Erie AVA is one of the largest grape-growing regions in the U.S., second only to California's Central Valley. Some top Lake Erie wine producers include Johnson Estate Winery, Mazza Vineyards, and South Shore Wine Company. Other prominent wineries in the region are Arrowhead Wine Cellars, Liberty Vineyards & Winery, and Quincy Cellars.

These wineries are known for their award-winning wines, and some are recognized as being among the largest or oldest producers in the region.

Champlain Valley of New York AVA

Signature Grapes: Marquette, La Crescent, Frontenac Established: 2016
Location: Northeastern NY, along Lake Champlain This is New York's newest AVA, focused on cold-hardy hybrids that can survive harsh northern winters. The wines are often crisp, floral, and distinctive in style, with a growing natural wine scene and a focus on small, family-run estates.
Fun Fact: Vineyards here regularly see winter lows of -30° F, making this one of the coldest wine-producing regions in North America.

Top **wine producers** in the Champlain Valley AVA include Four Maples Vineyard & Winery and Vesco Ridge Vineyards. While other highly-regarded New York producers like Weis Vineyards and Rose Hill Vineyards have won recent awards, they are located in different regions like the Finger Lakes and Long Island, respectively, not the Champlain Valley.

Niagara Escarpment AVA

Signature Grapes: Riesling, Cabernet Franc, Pinot Gris Established: 2005
Location: Western NY, near Niagara Falls
This small AVA benefits from moderate lake influence and elevated limestone-rich soils, supporting cool-climate viticulture. Although lesser known, the region has high potential for premium Riesling and red hybrid wines.
Fun Fact: The Niagara Escarpment is a geological formation that runs from New York to Wisconsin—it even shapes the cliffs over Niagara Falls!

Some top New York producers in the Niagara Escarpment AVA include Arrowhead Spring Vineyards, Chateau Niagara Winery, Freedom Run Winery, and Vizcarra Vineyards at Becker Farms. These wineries are known for producing a variety of wines that are well-regarded and reflect the region's unique climate and terroir.
Arrowhead Spring Vineyards: Frequently mentioned, the winery is noted for its sustainable practices and quality wines, such as its Arrowhead Red.

Chateau Niagara Winery: A consistently listed producer within the AVA.
Freedom Run Winery: Often highlighted as a top destination in the region.
Vizcarra Vineyards at Becker Farms: Known for producing a range of wines, including a notable Pinot Noir and Traminette.
Schulze Vineyards & Winery: Another frequently cited producer within the AVA.
Leonard Oakes Estate Winery: Mentioned for its wines, including a Skin Fermented White.
Long Cliff Vineyard & Winery: Recognized for its wines, such as a Dry Riesling and a Sauvignon Blanc.

95

Summary Table: New York Wine Regions

Region	Known For	Signature Grapes
Finger Lakes	Cool-climate whites & reds	Riesling, Cab Franc, Gewürztraminer
Long Island	Bordeaux-style blends & Chard	Merlot, Cabernet Franc, Chardonnay
Hudson River Region	Historic vineyards & hybrids	Seyval Blanc, Cab Franc, Chardonnay
Lake Erie	Juice grapes + hybrids	Concord, Chambourcin, Riesling

Region	Known For	Signature Grapes
Champlain Valley of NY	Cold-hardy, emerging AVA	Marquette, La Crescent, Frontenac
Niagara Escarpment	Minerality & elevation	Riesling, Pinot Gris, and hybrids

96

New York Wine & Food Pairing Guide

Finger Lakes AVA

Pairing Ideas:
Dry Riesling: Seared scallops with lemon-butter sauce or Thai green papaya salad
Off-dry Riesling: Spicy Indian curry or pork chops with fruit compote
Chardonnay: Roasted chicken with tarragon and mushrooms
Cabernet Franc: Grilled eggplant, lentil stew, or duck breast with berry sauce
Why it works: The high acidity and mineral tones in these wines balance spice, fat, and freshness beautifully.

Long Island AVA

Pairing Ideas:
Merlot: Mushroom risotto, roasted lamb, or meatloaf with herbs

Cabernet Franc: Charred vegetable lasagna or grilled sausage
Sauvignon Blanc: Goat cheese salad, oysters, or grilled asparagus
Chardonnay: Lobster roll with lemon aioli or creamy pasta.
Why it works: Long Island wines are supple, elegant, and balanced— ideal for fresh coastal fare and seasonal produce.

Hudson River Region AVA

Pairing Ideas:
Seyval Blanc: Quiche Lorraine, herb-roasted chicken, or soft cheeses
Chardonnay: Shrimp and grits or baked brie
Baco Noir: Barbecued ribs or shepherd's pie
Cabernet Franc: Mushroom ravioli or venison stew
Why it works: The cooler climate yields wines with a savory edge, perfect for pairing with earthy, hearty dishes.

Lake Erie AVA (Shared with Ohio & Pennsylvania)

Pairing Ideas:
Vidal Blanc (Late Harvest): Peach tart or blue cheese with honey

Riesling: Sweet-and-sour glazed salmon
Concord (Sweet Red): Chocolate cake or peanut butter truffles
Why it works: Sweet and aromatic wines pair well with salty, spicy, or dessert dishes.

Niagara Escarpment AVA

Pairing Ideas:
Ice Wine (Vidal): Foie gras, blue cheese, or apple tarte tatin
Riesling: Smoked trout or pork schnitzel
Cabernet Franc: Roast turkey with cranberry relish.
Why it works: These wines offer purity, structure, and sweetness that enhance bold, sweet-savory, or rich foods.

97

Quick Cheat Sheet: New York Wine & Food Pairing

Wine Style	Try With...	Regions
Dry Riesling	Shellfish, pork, Thai food	Finger Lakes, Niagara Escarpment
Off Dry to Sweet Riesling	Indian curry, glazed meats, fruit-based dishes	Finger Lakes, Lake Erie
Chardonnay	Roast chicken, seafood, creamy sauces	Finger Lakes, Long Island
Cabernet Franc	Grilled vegetables, duck, gamey meats	Long Island, Hudson Valley
Merlot	Lamb, mushroom-based dishes	Long Island

Wine Style	Try With...	Regions
Sauvignon Blanc	Goat cheese, oysters, asparagus	Long Island
Hybrid (Baco, Seyval, Concord)	BBQ, comfort foods, desserts	Hudson Valley, Lake Erie
Ice Wine (Vidal)	Foie gras, pungent cheese, fruit desserts	Niagara Escarpment

98

Wine Laws

Wine has always been more than just a beverage. It is geography in a glass, history you can taste, and—at its core—an expression of people and place. But how do we ensure that a bottle labeled "Champagne" comes from the Champagne region? Or that a "Chianti" carries the soul of Tuscany in every sip? The answer lies in a complex web of wine laws—a global framework designed to protect not just brands and markets, but also centuries of tradition, biodiversity, and regional identity.

Global wine laws are both practical and poetic. On one hand, they regulate grape varieties, production methods, and labeling standards. On the other hand, they serve as guardians of cultural heritage, ensuring that wines from a particular region remain true to their origins. From the tightly defined Appellations d'Origine Contrôlée of France to the flexible American Viticultural Areas in the United States, these systems vary widely in structure, strictness, and philosophy.

This chapter examines the major wine classification systems worldwide—how they originated, how they operate, and why they are significant. We'll discuss how Europe's centuries-old laws compare with the transparency of the New World, and how emerging regions are shaping their own legal identities. You'll also discover why some names, like

"Port" or "Prosecco" are fiercely protected, and why others, like "Shiraz" or "Riesling," travel freely across borders.

Whether you're a wine lover, a legal nerd, or an advocate for indigenous grapes and honest labeling, understanding global wine law offers a deeper appreciation for what's in your glass. Behind every label lies not just a vineyard, but a vision, a contract, and often, a centuries-old story that someone fought to protect.

France – Appellation d'Origine Contrôlée (AOC)

AOC (Appellation d'Origine Contrôlée): Must follow rigid rules about grape types, yields, winemaking methods, and origin.
IGP (Indication Géographique Protégée): Region-specific but allows more flexibility.
Vin de France: National table wine with no regional claim.
Protected Names: Champagne, Bordeaux, Burgundy, Chablis, Sancerre
Why it matters: Protects cultural heritage and ensures wine reflects its origin.

Italy – DOC / DOCG System

DOC (Denominazione di Origine Controllata): Regulates the region, grape variety, and method.
DOCG (Denominazione di Origine Controllata e Garantita): The highest tier, with even more scrutiny, often blind-tasted before approval.
IGT (Indicazione Geografica Tipica): More freedom to blend or experiment.
Vino da Tavola: Table wine without geographic designation.
Protected Names: Chianti, Barolo, Prosecco, Brunello, Amarone
Fun Fact: "Super Tuscans" started as rebellious IGT wines!

Greece - PDO / PGI System

PDO (Protected Designation of Origin / ΠΟΠ):
The top tier. Specific grapes from specific places (e.g., Santorini Assyrtiko, Naoussa Xinomavro). PGI (Protected Geographical Indication / ΠΓΕ):
More flexible but still regional. Think fun blends, modern styles. Table Wine (Epitrapezios Oinos): No regional or varietal requirements—drink local and casual.
Protected Names: Santorini, Nemea, Naoussa, Mantinia
Fun Fact: Greece's wine laws are rooted in EU standards, but they're also protecting grapes that have been cultivated for over 3,000 years—think of it as bureaucratic mythology.

Spain – Denominación de Origen (DO)

DO (Denominación de Origen): Controls grape varieties, yields, and origin.
DOCa (Denominación de Origen Calificada): Elite status— only Rioja and Priorat have it.
Vino de la Tierra: Like IGT—flexible, regionally labeled.
Vino de Mesa: Table wine.
Spain also labels aging levels (unique!):
Crianza (min. 1 year aging),
Reserva (3 years),
Gran Reserva (5+ years)

Portugal – Denominação de Origem Protegida (DOP)

DOP (Denominação de Origem Protegida): Like France's AOC. IGP (Indicação Geográfica Protegida): Looser rules.
Vinho: Table wine category.
Protected Names: Port, Madeira, Vinho Verde, Dão Fortified wines like Port and Madeira have their own regulatory bodies (IVDP, IVM).

Germany – Prädikatswein System

Qualitätswein (QbA): Quality wine from approved regions.
Prädikatswein: Higher tier, classified by grape ripeness at harvest:

Kabinett, Spätlese, Auslese, Beerenauslese, Trockenbeerenauslese, Eiswein
Landwein: Like IGP
Tafelwein: Table wine
Ripeness = sweetness potential.
Germany loves precision and Riesling.
Bonus: "Trocken" = dry, "Halbtrocken" = off-dry.

Austria – DAC System

DAC (Districtus Austriae Controllatus): Austria's answer to France's AOC. Focuses on typicity, grape, and regional style (e.g., Kamptal DAC = Grüner or Riesling only).
Qualitätswein: Quality wine from a specific region; must pass chemical and sensory analysis.
Prädikatswein: Sweetness-based classification for late-harvest and dessert wines (e.g., Beerenauslese, Trockenbeerenauslese).
Landwein & Tafelwein: Regional or table wines with fewer restrictions.
Protected Names: Wachau, Kamptal, Kremstal, Burgenland Fun Fact: Austria's strict wine laws were revamped in the 1980s after a scandal—now they're some of the toughest in the world, and their wines are better than ever.

South America - Chile & Argentina's Wine Laws

Argentina

IG (Indicación Geográfica): Defines the larger region (e.g., Mendoza).
DOC (Denominación de Origen Controlada): Rare but prestigious (e.g., Luján de Cuyo).
Varietal Labeling: Must be 85% of the stated grape.
Protected Names: Luján de Cuyo, San Rafael
Fun Fact: Malbec's revival in Argentina was so successful, the country made it a national symbol—and has its own Malbec World Day (April 17).

Chile

DO (Denominación de Origen): Covers geographic zones (e.g., Maipo, Colchagua).
Labeling Laws: 75% of the grapes must be from the labeled varietal, vintage, and region, but many producers voluntarily meet the 85% standard for exports.
Climate Zones: Costa (coastal), Entre Cordilleras (valley),
and Andes—indicating growing conditions.
Protected Names: Maipo Valley, Casablanca, Colchagua
Fun Fact: Chile's vineyards are phylloxera-free, thanks to natural geographic isolation, making

it one of the purest viticultural environments on Earth.

United States - AVA System (American Viticultural Areas)

AVA (American Viticultural Area): Geographic zones like Napa Valley or Willamette Valley.
No rules on grapes, yields, or method—just where it's from.
Labeling Laws: If it says a grape (e.g., "Cabernet Sauvignon"), it must contain at least 75% of it

If it lists an AVA, at least 85% of the grapes must come from that area. Bonus: California "Champagne" and "Port" are still allowed under old agreements—but new producers can't use those terms.

Australia - GI System (Geographical Indications)

GI (Geographical Indication): Defines origin only— not method or variety.
Strict on labeling: At least 85% of the grapes must be from the specified place or variety.
No hierarchy like AOC/DOC—but very consumer-transparent.

Australia helped popularize varietal labeling (E.g., Shiraz, Chardonnay).

New Zealand - Geographical Indication (GI)

Same GI system as Australia.
NZ wines must be 100% grown in NZ to be labeled as such. Major GIs: Marlborough, Central Otago, Hawke's Bay.
Famous for Sauvignon Blanc, but Pinot Noir and Syrah are rising stars.

South Africa - Wine of Origin (WO) System

WO (Wine of Origin): Indicates the precise location— region, district, or even single vineyard
(e.g., Stellenbosch, Swartland).
Label Requirements: To list a vintage, variety, or origin, 85% of the wine must come from that element.
Estate Wine: All grapes must be grown and vinified on the same estate.
Protected Names: Pinotage (native variety), Constantia, Stellenbosch, Robertson
Fun Fact: South Africa's WO system was introduced in 1973— modeled after European AOC laws, but adapted for a young, diverse wine industry.

What All These Systems Have in Common:

Feature	Why It Matters
Place of Origin (Terroir)	Wines must reflect their geography
Grape Rules	Some regions only allow particular grapes
Production Rules	Aging, yield, and method can be regulated
Label Protection	"Champagne" or "Chianti" can't be misused
Consumer Trust	Ensures authenticity and quality

Made in United States
North Haven, CT
09 December 2025

84187046R00172